EXPLORING ADVANCED TECHNOLOGIES FOR THE

Future Combat Systems Program

john **MATSUMURA**

randall **STEEB**

tom **HERBERT**

john **GORDON**

carl **RHODES**

russell **GLENN**

michael **BARBERO**

fred **GELLERT**

phyllis **KANTAR**

gail **HALVERSON**

robert **COCHRAN**

paul **STEINBERG**

Prepared for the United States Army

ARROYO CENTER

RAND

Approved for public release; distribution unlimited

The research described in this report was sponsored by the United States Army under Contract DASW01-96-C-0004.

Library of Congress Cataloging-in-Publication Data

Exploring advanced technologies for the future combat systems program / John Matsumura ... [et al.].
  p. cm.
  Includes bibliographical references.
  "MR-1332."
  ISBN 0-8330-3026-4
  1. United States. Army. 2. Armored vehicles, Military—United States. 3. Tank warfare—Effect of technological innovations on. 4. Combat—Effect of technological innovations on 5. Military planning—United States. I. Matsumura, John.

UE160 .E97 2002
358'.1883—dc21

2001041628

RAND is a nonprofit institution that helps improve policy and decisionmaking through research and analysis. RAND® is a registered trademark. RAND's publications do not necessarily reflect the opinions or policies of its research sponsors.

© Copyright 2002 RAND

All rights reserved. No part of this book may be reproduced in any form by any electronic or mechanical means (including photocopying, recording, or information storage and retrieval) without permission in writing from RAND.

Published 2002 by RAND
1700 Main Street, P.O. Box 2138, Santa Monica, CA 90407-2138
1200 South Hayes Street, Arlington, VA 22202-5050
201 North Craig Street, Suite 102, Pittsburgh, PA 15213
RAND URL: http://www.rand.org/
To order RAND documents or to obtain additional information, contact Distribution Services: Telephone: (310) 451-7002;
Fax: (310) 451-6915; Email: order@rand.org

PREFACE

This report summarizes the research findings of a short-time-frame study conducted by RAND Arroyo Center to support the Army Science Board (ASB) Summer Study 2000, "Technical and Tactical Opportunities for Revolutionary Advances in Rapidly Deployable Joint Ground Forces in the 2015–2020 Era." The purpose of the RAND research was to explore a range of advanced technologies for potential contribution to the Future Combat Systems program; it is intended to be a think piece and is not a guide to the contractors charged with designing the Future Combat Systems. This research represents only one part of the ASB study, focusing specifically on force effectiveness in a notional small-scale contingency and on the associated spectrum of challenges that such a situation might entail. In conducting the study, the research team interacted with various members of the ASB, drawing extensively on their forward-looking ideas and ultimately integrating many of them into the research. High-resolution combat modeling and simulation was used to assess many key aspects of force performance, environmental factors, and system-of-systems interactions within the context of the scenario.

This work should be of interest to defense policymakers, military technologists, and concept developers.

This research was conducted in the Force Development and Technology Program of RAND Arroyo Center. The Arroyo Center is a federally funded research and development center sponsored by the United States Army.

For more information on RAND Arroyo Center, contact the Director of Operations (telephone 310-393-0411, extension 6500; FAX 310-451-6952; e-mail donnab@rand.org), or visit the Arroyo Center's Web site at *http://www.rand.org/organization/ard/*.

CONTENTS

Preface iii
Figures ix
Tables xi
Summary xiii
Acknowledgments xxi
Acronyms xxiii

Chapter One
   INTRODUCTION 1
   Background 1
   Objective 2
   Approach 4
      Select Concepts and Technologies to Be Assessed 4
      Modify an Existing Scenario 4
      Determine How to Integrate Future Concepts and
         Technologies into Simulation and Run the
         Simulation 6
   Organization of This Document 9

Chapter Two
   HOW MUCH REMOTE "SITUATIONAL
   UNDERSTANDING" IS ACHIEVABLE IN THE 2015–
   2020 TIME FRAME? 11
   What Remote Intelligent Capabilities Are Likely to Be
      Available in the Time Frame? 12

How Much Situational Understanding Can These Remote
Assets Provide? 15

Chapter Three
WHAT CAN BE ACCOMPLISHED USING A FULL RANGE
OF JOINT ASSETS WITHOUT CLOSE COMBAT? 21
How Do Remote and Tactical (Organic) Sensor Networks
Perform? 22
How Do Long-Range Fire Systems Perform? 25
What Are the Effects of Long-Range Fires on
Noncombatants? 28

Chapter Four
DOES ADDING GROUND MANEUVER, POSSIBLY CLOSE
COMBAT, WITH THE BCT OFFER ADVANTAGES? 33
How Might a Future BCT Be Structured, and How Would
It Be Used?................................. 33
How Does the Baseline Force Fare? 36
How Can Baseline Performance Be Improved? 38
Observations on the Use of Ground Forces 44

Chapter Five
WHAT ARE THE IMPLICATIONS OF ENHANCED AIR
INSERTION OF THE BCT, SUCH AS BY
VERTICAL ENVELOPMENT? 47
What Would the Airlifter Look Like? 48
What Is the Vertical Envelopment Mission? 48
What Are the Results of the Vertical Envelopment
Mission? 51
How Survivable Is the FTR in the Vertical Envelopment
Mission? 53

Chapter Six
CONCLUSIONS................................ 59
Key Observations 59
Potential Enemy Countermeasures 60
Countermeasures Against Long-Range Fires (Remote
Attack)................................... 60
Countermeasures Against BCT Ground Attack 61
Countermeasures Against Vertical Envelopment
Attack 61
Recommendations 62

Appendix: NONCOMBATANT CASUALTIES AS A RESULT OF
    ALLIED ENGAGEMENTS   65

Bibliography   77

FIGURES

1.1.	JANUS Screen Image of Serbian BGs	6
1.2.	TOE for Serbian BG	7
1.3.	High-Resolution Modeling and Simulation Network at RAND	8
2.1.	Remote Intelligence Assets Available in the Time Frame	13
2.2.	Example of Targets Detected Through Foliage	16
2.3.	Comparison of Current and FOPEN Capabilities Versus Ground Truth	17
2.4.	Scene of Glodane Village in Kosovo in 1999 Taken by Remote Assets	18
3.1.	Examples of Organic Sensing Assets Used	23
3.2.	Sensor Network Performance	24
3.3.	Parametric Weapon Performance	27
3.4.	Capabilities of Advanced Technologies Weapons to Kill Stationary Targets	28
3.5.	Illustration of Noncombatant Effects of Dropping Four 250-Pound JDAM with 3-Meter TLE	29
4.1.	Notional BCT Structure Assumed for the ASB Study	34
4.2.	Illustration of Baseline Ground Maneuver Operation for BCT	35
4.3.	Kills and Losses by Type or Class of System in Baseline Case	37
4.4a.	BCT Kills of Red Systems in the Baseline Case	38
4.4b.	BCT Losses of Blue Systems in the Baseline Case	39
4.5.	Key Technologies Used to Improve BCT Performance	40

4.6.	Kills and Losses by Type or Class of System in the Best Performance Case	43
4.7.	Red and Blue Attrition for Improved BCT Case	44
5.1.	Notional Image of One FTR Concept	48
5.2.	Three Potential Landing Zones for the Vertical Envelopment Mission	49
5.3.	Associated Group Maneuver of BCT Units in Force Envelopment Mission	50
5.4.	Kills and Losses by System for Best FTR Case with Vertical Envelopment	53
5.5.	Location of Red and Blue Attrition in the Vertical Envelopment Mission	54
5.6.	The SA-15 and 2S6 Systems	55
5.7.	The SA-14/18 MANPADS and AAA Systems	56
5.8.	Representation of Air Defense Coverage	57
5.9.	Possible Alternative to Vertical Envelopment but Still Using Ground Maneuver	58

TABLES

2.1.	Expected Performance Levels of Remote Assets	14
4.1.	Outcomes of Different Technology Excursions	41
5.1.	Outcomes of Flexible Air Insertion, Assuming 100 Percent Survivability	52

SUMMARY

The U.S. Army has begun adapting to transform itself to meet the needs of the new millennium. This transformation vision will ultimately lead to a more responsive Army capable of full-spectrum operations. As a starting point for realizing this vision, the Army is configuring a new kind of mechanized force—a medium-weight force that is highly mobile and can be air-deployed around the globe in a matter of days. As the Army begins its transformation into medium-weight forces, it will do so in two integrated steps, starting with an Interim Force and ending with an Objective Force with a first unit equipped in the next decade or so. The cornerstone for this Objective Force will be the Future Combat Systems (FCS)—a network-centric system of systems, which will involve developing a new family of medium-weight vehicles. Understanding the capabilities and challenges of the Objective Force built around the FCS concept is critical for the Army.

To help achieve this understanding, the 2000 Army Science Board (ASB) was tasked to examine "Technical and Tactical Opportunities for Revolutionary Advances in Rapidly Deployable Joint Ground Forces in the 2015–2020 Era." RAND Arroyo Center was asked to help the ASB assess the many technologies, tactics, and operational concepts being considered for the rapid-reaction transformation, with a focus on their application to small-scale contingencies (SSCs). By modifying an existing SSC scenario developed for Army research and using the constituent modeling capabilities provided by its unique simulation environment, the Arroyo Center focused on answering four research questions:

- How much remote "situational understanding" is achievable in the 2015–2020 time frame?
- What can be accomplished using a full range of joint assets without close combat (manned)?
- Does adding ground maneuver, possibly close combat, with the brigade combat team (BCT) offer advantages?
- What are the implications of enhanced air insertion of the BCT, such as vertical envelopment?

RESEARCH FINDINGS

Our research findings fundamentally consist of answers to the above questions. Given the relatively short time frame allowed for this study, and in particular for those questions requiring simulation-based modeling, very little sensitivity analysis was achievable. As a result, the answers provided below are conditional on key assumptions, which show up as caveats to the analysis throughout this document.

Answer 1: Remote Assets Will Not Ensure "Understanding" on the Future Battlefield

Although significant strides are clearly being made in remote reconnaissance, intelligence, surveillance, and target acquisition capability out to year 2020 and beyond, our initial assessment suggests that such capabilities, even if pursued aggressively, cannot alone ensure adequate situational understanding.[1] The physical environment (e.g., weather, foliage), the presence of noncombatants, and the countermeasure options available to an adversary (especially within the representative SSC used in this research) all provide challenges and complications that limit what can be accomplished from afar. Even rapidly improving foliage-penetrating (FOPEN) radar and

---

[1] Remote assets as defined here include medium- and high-altitude and space-based assets. Excluded are ground-based sensors such as robotic sensors and distributed sensor networks. Although we examined a large suite of remote assets, this was not a comprehensive set. It is possible that other technologies can improve the picture, but there will likely be a range of countermeasures.

hyperspectral sensing cannot guarantee detection. In many ways, the SSC's fundamental nature exacerbates these factors as compared to a major theater war (MTW) (e.g., the need to distinguish between noncombatants and adversaries may be typical for the SSC-level operation).

Answer 2: Advanced Remote Application of Firepower Can Produce Attrition, but Considerable Collateral Damage Is Likely

The second research question asks to what extent the mission can be accomplished without resorting to ground forces. Because the remote sensors provide only a partial understanding of the situation, we added (with ASB input) a sophisticated tactical sensor network deemed achievable in the 2015–2020 time frame that included advanced distributed sensors, tactical unmanned aerial vehicles (UAVs), and special hovering UAVs. All systems incorporate advanced sensor technologies that would be cued by the full range of remote assets, including FOPEN radar, available in the 2015–2020 time frame.

With this sensor network capability, along with major advances in precision-guided weaponry, as many as one-third of all enemy forces can be engaged and, with highly aggressive application of precision-guided standoff weapons, ultimately attrited. However, such an aggressive use of even the most advanced precision-guided weaponry is likely to come at the cost of significant noncombatant losses and collateral damage. Our estimates, based on population densities of the region during the early days of the SSC scenario we studied, conservatively suggest at least a few thousand casualties, either injured or killed.[2]

Furthermore, despite the high levels of attrition suffered by enemy forces, our analysis suggests that such standoff capability will not ensure accomplishment of the military mission in the SSC, as defined by the scenario. The fundamental reason is the inability to decisively

---

[2]The Appendix contains the details of a methodology used to estimate casualties; data for the methodology were based on civilian behavior and flow rates during the early phases of Operation Allied Force.

stop the ingress of enemy units; thus, enemy presence can be reinforced over time. Finally, based on historical evidence seen in the event that is the basis of the scenario we studied, countermeasures would most likely be implemented to reduce the effectiveness of both sensors and weapons associated with standoff attacks.

Answer 3: Using Ground Forces Allows the Mission to Be Accomplished but with Some Losses

To answer the third question about the contribution of a ground force attack, we used a notional brigade combat team (BCT) and applied the force to the scenario using current doctrine, tactics, techniques, and procedures.[3] In this context, the BCT must enter through mountain passes, with the objective of evicting the in-place forces and blocking follow-on reinforcements. Generally, we found that the mission can be accomplished, but with some cost. Since the enemy has the terrain, preparation, and cover, the notional BCT is at a great disadvantage from the onset.

Since an Active Protection System (APS) was identified as one of the BCT's key enabling technologies, we evaluated the BCT performance both with and without this capability. In both cases, we then added different versions of robotic vehicles to be used in the high-risk, reconnaissance mission: the first was an unarmed robotic vehicle, equipped with a second-generation mast-mounted forward-looking infrared, that was linked to an FCS direct-fire vehicle; the second was an armed robotic vehicle that would engage with its own notional direct-fire weapon; and the third was an armed robotic vehicle equipped with muzzle-flash detection, which would permit engagement without the need to recognize the target. Finally, we included a case that included long-range fires. The simulation shows that the most dramatic effect is adding the long-range fires capability to all the other added capabilities, which raised the loss-exchange ratio from the baseline 1.25 in the no-APS case (1.59 in the APS case) to 4.04 and 4.87, respectively; however, the addition of long-range fires did result in over a thousand noncombatant casualties.

_____

[3] Because there was not an approved operational and organizational construct for the BCT, we used best-estimate inputs for our research.

Answer 4: Successful Vertical Envelopment Transforms the Mission from Offense to Defense

The last research question involved assessing the utility of the Future Transport Rotorcraft (FTR) to operationally insert the notional BCT. Here, the ASB selected landing zones well into hostile territory. This aggressive action changes the fight from a more traditional ground maneuver into a nonlinear engagement, with the BCT threatening from different positions. Not only did the use of the FTR provide flexibility to leverage intelligence, terrain, and positioning, the insertion also transformed the Blue force mission from an offensive action to a defensive one. If successful insertion is assumed (which is not resolved at this time), this capability results in a much more favorable outcome.

Despite the protection systems that are becoming available for aircraft, the asymmetric nature of the air defense threat to aircraft suggests that significantly more improvements will be needed to enable this kind of mission. As an alternative, the FTR or C-130Js (with modification) could be used to deploy forces forward, and these ground forces could then maneuver under the enemy air defense umbrella to their objective. This could result in an outcome as favorable as the one achieved with vertical envelopment.

CONCLUSIONS

Given the strong influence that SSC-related factors impose on combat and its conduct in the future, it follows that as the Army redesigns itself to respond out 15 to 20 years, these factors should be integrated into the design process. This study represents only a beginning part of this challenging process.

Key Observations

In summary, we found that an enemy who relies on cover, concealment, deception, intermingling, and dispersion will be very difficult to monitor from overhead assets (even in the 2015–2020 time frame of the analysis). While combined uses of organic, tactical sensors and remote assets show much promise in finding enemy assets, these systems tend to become much more constrained in areas with dense foliage. While advances in remote precision firepower will probably be able to provide some level of attrition (e.g., small smart bombs), attrition by itself will not necessarily accomplish the mission. The enemy can still reinforce, possibly at a faster rate than the attrition. Further, risk to noncombatants and collateral damage considerations may limit the use of such fires in many instances. These factors combined highlight the need for some level of presence on the ground.

When traditional maneuver (through the current doctrine) with the notional BCT is used, the mission is accomplished, but with some losses; with the wide range of advanced technologies available in the time frame, losses can be reduced, but perhaps not by enough. New and novel, perhaps even nontraditional, doctrine and tactics will most likely be required to ensure success in putting a force based on 20-ton vehicles against a traditional heavy armor threat.

Flexible air insertion shows much promise, but this also can carry great risk. Such expedient operational maneuver capability offered by a FTR can change the dynamics of battle by allowing a force to get into key positions before they are contested. As a result, less predictable offensive tactics can be used, and forward-based defensive strong points can be established. However, survivability of such aircraft is not yet resolved, which places a high priority on the development of multispectral protection systems should this capability be implemented.

Potential Enemy Countermeasures

The obvious question facing any long-term technology improvement program is what the enemy can do to counter it. The responses range from deception to direct attack on vulnerable systems and range across those directed at long-range fires (remote attack), those directed against a BCT ground attack, and those directed at a vertical envelopment attack. In terms of the first use, countermeasures—such as hiding well within tree lines or covered urban areas but with good line of sight (LOS) and field of fire—can be especially effective when the Blue forces are relying on standoff sensors and long-range fires. In addition, the deceptions do not have to be perfect; techniques that save a few more units, personnel, and equipment can lead to more Blue losses later during ground attack options. Moreover, the techniques are relatively inexpensive and readily available or producible.

Countermeasures against the notional BCT ground attack include using extensive combined arms "strong point" (especially in urban areas with noncombatants) and "hardening" targets, preparing infantry and armor "dug-in" ambush positions, using cover and concealment during the resupply movement, and calling on cannons, mortars, and multiple rocket launchers for fire support. Although these techniques are labor-intensive and require time and resources to implement, they can readily be accomplished by even poor armies.

Finally, the enemy's attack of FTR lift assets is particularly dangerous for the Blue force. Simulation runs showed the Blue force losing most of the FTR fleet to the enemy's robust air defense. Particular countermeasures include locating air defense artillery assets to destroy the FTR during both ingress and egress, attacking landing zones with long-range artillery, and attacking Blue forces from multiple directions to cut forces off.

RECOMMENDATIONS

Although it is not necessarily obvious, an SSC can in some ways be more complex to conduct than an MTW. As we observed in the context of this research, the capability to accomplish military objectives may come second to the conditions and constraints imposed by the SSC itself. As a result, even 15 to 20 years out, the available suite of remote sensors and precision-guided weapons is not a panacea; indeed, even if such forecasted remote capabilities had been available in 1999, many of the challenges seen in the event that defined our scenario would have been the same.

A new medium-weight force, such as the notional BCT considered here, represents a more direct method for responding to such challenges, providing a means for direct tactical target engagement with the ability to discriminate noncombatants. However, we note that having the ability to deploy rapidly, in and of itself, may not be enough. Other measures may be needed.

For one, policy may need to be adjusted to reflect the capability of the unit itself. That is, having the capability to deploy quickly may ultimately mean very little if the decision to use the force covers a lengthy period. Thus, if policy and guidelines are not integrated with the new capability, they may become the constraining factor. Such policy issues should be researched further.

For another, to be successful the BCT may have to have contain various technology enhancements. The key technologies identified for the notional BCT in this research were intelligence systems and tactical sensor networks; robotics-related technologies, such as advanced UAVs and unmanned ground vehicles; weapons (both direct and indirect) that can engage through foliage; and protection systems for ground and air vehicles. These can provide considerable and needed improvement toward BCT mission effectiveness.

The most favorable outcomes, however, occurred when a joint force was used—specifically, when ground forces such as the BCT were complemented with a range of appropriate remote sensors and weapons. Although casualties are likely with the aggressive use of remote weapons, the presence of a ground force can help to mitigate this. Similarly, ground forces, without the "softening" effect of standoff engagement, were more susceptible to being ambushed and engaged by heavy armor.

We emphasize that the SSC examined here is only one of many situations that should be considered when evaluating major acquisition decisions. Other scenarios and missions should be explored in a wide range of locations. In addition, we note that in this quick-response study, only a handful of key technology areas were ultimately examined and assessed. This set should certainly be expanded to include the many other ideas being generated. Although there will most likely be a continuing desire to resolve the SSC class of crises through remote application of force, many of the tactics and technologies associated with these kinds of engagements come with major limitations, and those limitations should be evaluated and understood more fully (and assessed with risk mitigation) as the Army and DARPA explore various joint concepts and designs for the Objective Force.

ACKNOWLEDGMENTS

The authors would like to thank the numerous individuals who generously contributed their time to this research effort. First and foremost, the authors must acknowledge the key contributions provided by the various members and affiliates of the Army Science Board. Outstanding guidance and, in some cases, support were provided by Dr. Robert Douglas, GEN(R) David Maddox, LTG(R) Charlie Otstott, and Major General Paul Pochmara. Additionally, we thank the following individuals for the many fascinating intellectual exchanges during the six-week study period, which helped to shape the research: Dr. Joseph Braddock, LTG(R) Butch Funk, GEN(R) Paul Gorman, Dr. Jasper Lupo, Dr. Fenner Milton, Dr. George Singley, and Dr. Anthony Tether.

Second, the authors wish to thank the following sponsors, who provided the foundation from which this research could be performed: from the Office of the Assistant Vice Chief of Staff of the Army, LTG David Byrnes, COL Phillip Coker, and LTC Timothy Muchmore; and from the Office of the Assistant Secretary of the Army for Acquisition, Logistics, and Technology, Dr. Michael Andrews, Dr. Lawrence Stotts, LTC Marion Van Fosson, and Dr. Pamela Beatrice.

Others who provided information in support of this research include Mr. Steve Percy, Mr. Dan Ericson, and Mr. Peter Burke from Picatinny Arsenal, who provided data on smart munition weapon performance and the value of various technology improvements; and LTC Tommy Kelley and MAJ Stephen Iwicki from V Corps ACE, who provided detailed information on enemy tactics and noncombatant casualties from Operation Allied Force.

Finally, the authors thank their RAND colleagues who shared their ideas and gave generously of their time: Dr. Marygail Brauner, MAJ Todd Key, MAJ Pat Kirk, Dr. Kenneth Horn, Mr. Gary McLeod, Dr. David Owen, Dr. Bruce Pirnie, Dr. John Pinder, and Dr. John Stillion. Dr. Myron Hura and Dr. Walter Perry, reviewers of this report, provided many thoughtful and insightful comments.

ACRONYMS

AA	Anti-Armor
AAA	Anti-Aircraft Artillery
AAN	Army After Next
ACE	Analysis and Control Element
AD	Air Defense
ADA	Air Defense Artillery
ADAS	Air Deliverable Acoustic Sensor
APC	Armored Personnel Carrier
APFSDS	Armor-Piercing Fin-Stabilized Discarding Sabot
APS	Active Protection System
ASA(ALT)	Assistant Secretary of the Army (Acquisition, Logistics, and Technology)
ASB	Army Science Board
ASP	Acoustic Sensor Program
ATR	Automatic Target Recognition
BCT	Brigade Combat Team
BG	Battle Group
C2	Command and Control

CAGIS	Cartographic Analysis and Geographic Information System
CEP	Circular Error Probable
CS	Combat Support
DRB	Division Ready Brigade
DTED	Digital Terrain Elevation Data
EFOG-M	Enhanced Fiber-Optic Guided Missile
E/O	Electro-optic
ESAMS	Enhanced Surface to Air Missile Simulation
ET	Electro-thermal
FCS	Future Combat Systems
FLIR	Forward-Looking Infrared
FOPEN	Foliage Penetration Radar
FTI	Fixed Target Indicator
FTR	Future Transport Rotorcraft
FUE	First Unit Equipped
GMTI	Ground Moving Target Indicator
GPS	Global Positioning System
HIMARS	High Mobility Artillery Rocket System
IBCT	Interim Brigade Combat Team
IR	Infrared
IREMBASS	Improved Remotely Emplaced Battlefield Sensor System
ISAR	Inverse Synthetic Aperture Radar
JANUS	Two-Sided Force-on-Force Ground Combat Model
JDAM	Joint Direct Attack Munition
JMEM	Joint Munition Effectiveness Manual

JSEAD	Joint Suppression of Enemy Air Defenses
JSF	Joint Strike Fighter
JSTARS	Joint Surveillance Target Attack Radar System
KE	Kinetic Energy
LAV	Light Armored Vehicle
LER	Loss Exchange Ratio
LOCAAS	Low Cost Autonomous Attack Submunition
LOS	Line of Sight
LOSAT	Line of Sight Anti-Tank
LZ	Landing Zone
MADAM	Model to Assess Damage to Armor with Munitions
MANPADS	Man-Portable Air Defense System
MLRS	Multiple Launch Rocket System
MRL	Multiple Rocket Launcher
MTI	Moving Target Indicator
MTW	Major Theater War
NIIRS	National Imagery Interpretation Rating Scale
NTC	National Training Center
PGM	Precision-Guided Munition
P_k	Probability of Kill
RF	Radio Frequency
RISTA	Reconnaissance, Intelligence, Surveillance, and Target Acquisition
RJARS	RAND's Jamming Aircraft and Radar Simulation
ROE	Rules of Engagement
RTAM	RAND's Target Acquisition Model
SAR	Synthetic Aperture Radar

SEAD	Suppression of Enemy Air Defenses
SEMINT	Seamless Model Interface
SFW	Sensor Fused Weapon
SLID	Small Low-Cost Interceptor Device
SPT	Support
SSC	Small-Scale Contingency
TLE	Target Location Error
TOE	Table of Equipment
TRADOC	Training and Doctrine Command
TTP	Tactics, Techniques, and Procedures
UAV	Unmanned Aerial Vehicle
UGV	Unmanned Ground Vehicle

Chapter One
INTRODUCTION

BACKGROUND

The U.S. Army has begun transforming itself to meet the needs of the new millennium. This transformation vision, as defined by both the Chief of Staff and Secretary of the Army, will ultimately lead to a more responsive Army capable of full-spectrum operations. As a starting point for realizing this vision, the Army is configuring a new kind of mechanized force, one that is highly mobile and capable of being air-deployed around the globe in a matter of days.[1] This new type of force—a "medium" or "medium weight" force—will incorporate attributes from both light and heavy forces, bridging the gap between current capabilities and those needed for tomorrow's battles by incorporating some of the strategic responsiveness of light forces while providing some of the protection and tactical mobility associated with heavy forces.[2]

As the Army begins its transformation into medium-weight forces, it will do so in two integrated steps. The first step involves crafting a medium-weight force from technology that is currently available, resulting in an Interim Force, with the first unit equipped (FUE) as early as fiscal year 2003; the second step will involve creating a new

---

[1] The goal is 96 hours for the first brigade to deploy and 120 hours for the first division to deploy.

[2] The more formal reference to such medium-weight forces is, for the near term, the Interim Force and, for the longer term, the Objective Force. These forces are envisioned to be structured into brigade-sized units called interim brigade combat teams (IBCT) and brigade combat teams (BCT), respectively.

medium-weight force from advanced technologies and a yet-to-be-determined chassis, resulting in the Objective Force with an FUE as early as fiscal year 2012.

The cornerstone for the Objective Force is the Future Combat Systems (FCS).[3] The FCS is envisioned to be a network-centric force that will integrate a range of technologies likely to be centered around a family of vehicles.[4] The major difference between the FCS family of vehicles and the current inventory of heavy combat vehicles will be in how they fight. Physically, these vehicles will weigh less than 20 tons—a considerable weight reduction compared to the M1 Abrams tank, which weighs 70 tons, the M2A3 version of the Bradley Fighting Vehicle, which weighs 33 tons, and the planned self-propelled howitzer, the Crusader, which may weigh somewhere around 40 tons.[5] As a result of this dramatic reduction in weight, the force may have to rely more on surprise, dispersion, and standoff with massed effects to achieve its goals.

Understanding the capabilities and challenges of the FCS concept is critical for the Army. To help achieve this understanding, the 2000 Army Science Board (ASB) was tasked to examine "Technical and Tactical Opportunities for Revolutionary Advances in Rapidly Deployable Joint Ground Forces in the 2015–2020 Era."

OBJECTIVE

This report summarizes the findings from a quick-response analytic support effort performed at RAND in coordination with the ASB effort. The principal objective of the research was to help the ASB assess the many technologies, tactics, and operational concepts being considered for the transformation. More specifically, by interacting

---

[3]The Light Armored Vehicle (LAV) III produced by GM Canada has been selected as the chassis for the Interim Force.

[4]Using a common chassis across the variety of vehicles will provide *economy of scale* effects in research, development, and acquisition; peacetime operations and maintenance; and battlefield logistics.

[5]The self-propelled howitzer and the resupply vehicle of Crusader were each intended to weigh 55 tons, but this has since been reduced to 40–45 tons. See J. Matsumura, R. Steeb, and J. Gordon, *Assessment of Crusader*, Santa Monica, CA: RAND, MR-930-A, 1998, for more information on the issue of weight.

with members of the ASB Operations panel,[6] four key research questions were identified:

1. How much remote "situational understanding" is achievable in the 2015–2020 time frame?
2. What can be accomplished using a full range of joint assets without close combat (manned)?
3. Does adding ground maneuver, possibly close combat, with the brigade combat team (BCT) offer advantages?
4. What are the implications of enhanced air insertion of the BCT, such as by vertical envelopment?

The first question examined the level of intelligence or "situational understanding" available without using ground organic assets. In effect, it examined whether the commander would be able to deduce enough information about enemy force composition, location, tactics, and intent through the use of overhead assets, such as satellites and manned and unmanned aircraft.

The second question looked at the option of standoff fires, without commitment of ground forces. Among the systems available in this time frame are air, ground, and naval precision weapons. Unmanned ground sensors, advanced fire support systems, and other robotic elements were also considered for this option.

The third question considered the synergistic use of maneuvering ground forces and standoff fires. The ground force is assumed to be organized in the combined arms form of a BCT (associated with the Objective Force rather than the Interim Force), with tactics, techniques, and procedures (TTPs) of non-line-of-sight (NLOS) engagement and close combat.

The fourth question explored one of the more aggressive uses for the BCT—deep air insertion and maneuver against the enemy's flanks and rear areas. This examines issues of survivability of the airlifters, advantages in time and position afforded by rapid maneuver, and special synergies between air and ground elements in the operation.

---

[6]The original terms of reference for the ASB effort divided the work into four panels: Operations, Intelligence, Sustainment, and Training.

This work is preliminary, but it was envisioned from the outset to provide quantitative insights on the potential benefits and risks of the various options being considered for future rapid-reaction forces.

APPROACH

In answering the four research questions, we followed a multistep process, described below.

Select Concepts and Technologies to Be Assessed

We started by coordinating with the ASB on selecting concepts and technologies to be assessed. There are many concepts and technologies the ASB is considering for future U.S. rapid-reaction forces, ranging from advanced sensors to new command and control (C2) systems to manned and robotic weapons platforms. Many of these are also being considered for the FCS program.

Modify an Existing Scenario

We then modified an existing scenario for a small-scale contingency (SSC) in close, foliated terrain, to reflect 2015–2020 threat capabilities. The emphasis on an SSC was intended to complement the TRADOC Analysis Center (TRAC) analysis of a Southwest Asia major theater war (MTW) in open terrain.

In this case, we revisited a Kosovo scenario based on the 1999 Kosovo conflict, which was used in research conducted for the Center for Land Warfare and the Assistant Secretary of the Army (Acquisition, Logistics, and Technology) (ASA(ALT)). These projects examined near-term (IBCT) and far-term (FCS) options for rapid-reaction forces, and the scenario—now modified—provided a suitable framework for examining the issues facing the ASB. The modified SSC scenario used Kosovo terrain and a modified Serbian order of battle (systems upgraded to reflect the 2015–2020 time frame).[7]

---

[7]While the terrain, road network, towns, and degree of foliation are specific to Kosovo, the scenario is also intended to be representative of SSCs that might occur in many different parts of the world.

The mission of the rapid-reaction force is to neutralize four in-place enemy battle groups (BGs) in a 40×40-kilometer region and block any follow-on forces from joining up with them. The situation is much more stressful than clean engagements in open terrain. The Serb BGs are in place and dispersed throughout the region, they use foliage and cover to maximum advantage, and they are able to hide among noncombatants. The Blue force cannot simply ignore or bypass the enemy positions, but must quickly stabilize the situation to halt ethnic cleansing, control key areas, and set the conditions for a follow-on attack (if needed).

Figure 1.1 shows a JANUS screen simulation of Serb strength early in the conflict.[8] (In this case, we are showing a notional situation 6–8 days after the initiation of hostilities in Kosovo.[9])

We assumed the four BGs were dug in with defensive positions (shown by red circles in the left screen image). Seven more supporting battle groups would attempt to join them (shown as red arrows moving along multiple avenues of approach), once they became aware that the mountain passes were being secured by Blue forces. Many of the dug-in systems are located in the tree lines and are stationary, with minimal signature. The other seven BGs in the north are moving but are often under cover.

The Serb force is assumed to be an improved version from what they actually had in 1999, as reflected in the Table of Organization and Equipment (TOE) shown in Figure 1.2.

Each BG is a combined arms unit on the order of a reinforced company. There are roughly eight tanks and twelve armored personnel carriers (APCs) per battle group. The tanks, a mix of T-72s and T-80s,

---

[8] JANUS is a high-resolution force-on-force ground combat simulation developed by the U.S. Army and modified at RAND for analysis.

[9] The representation of this 2020 Serb force differs somewhat from the situation in 1999. In 1999, for example, Serb regular and paramilitary forces were rather evenly distributed throughout the province to fight the KLA and conduct ethnic cleansing. Small groups of enemy (platoons and companies) were operating in all areas of Kosovo. The enemy array used for this scenario assumes that to the rear of the four forward battle groups defending the passes, there are few enemy forces. The reinforcing battle groups shown as arrows are held off the map until U.S. forces start to arrive in our simulation.

6   Exploring Technologies for the Future Combat Systems Program

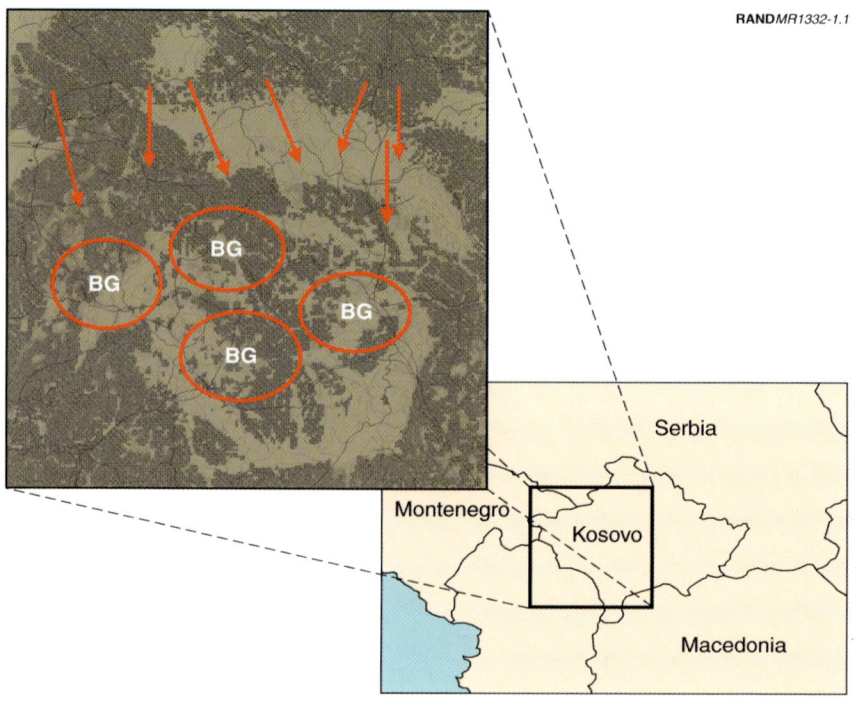

Figure 1.1—JANUS Screen Image of Serbian BGs

are equipped with forward-looking infrared (FLIRs) and AT-8 missiles with a 5-kilometer range. BTR-60 APCs have FLIRs and AT-6 missiles.

Determine How to Integrate Future Concepts and Technologies into Simulation and Run the Simulation

Figure 1.3 shows the constituent models of the simulation environment. The models are linked together using the Seamless Model Interface (SEMINT), a form of locally distributed network. The individual models center on the force-on-force JANUS wargaming simulation and comprise a wide range of capabilities. JANUS itself has been modified for analysis from its original form, by increasing the

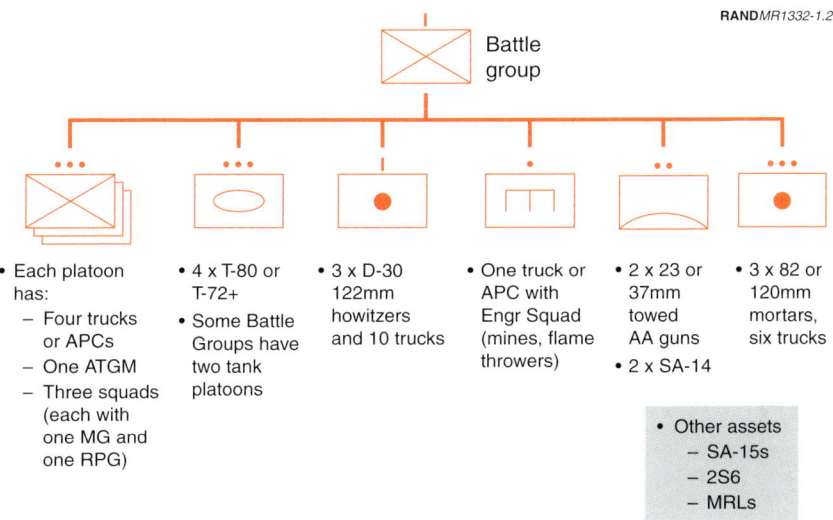

Figure 1.2—TOE for Serbian BG

size and scope of engagements, adding automated operations, and allowing special digital terrain representations.

The other models surrounding JANUS are primarily for modeling advanced systems. RAND Jamming and Radar Model (RJARS) dynamically simulates infrared (IR) and radio frequency (RF) air defense engagements against helicopters, unmanned aerial vehicle (UAVs), and fixed-wing aircraft. Model to Assess Damage to Armor with Munitions (MADAM) models the flyout, encounter, detection, and endgame with smart and brilliant munitions. The combination of the RAND Target Acquisition Model (RTAM) and the Cartographic Analysis and Geographic Information System (CAGIS) enables us to represent detailed target detection/acquisition phenomenology as needed, including low-observable vehicles. The Acoustic Sensor Program (ASP) models acoustic sensor phenomenology. And the Active Protection System (APS) simulates the effectiveness of vehicle protection systems against a variety of incoming weapons. Preliminary communications and C2 models represent the connectivity and

8   Exploring Technologies for the Future Combat Systems Program

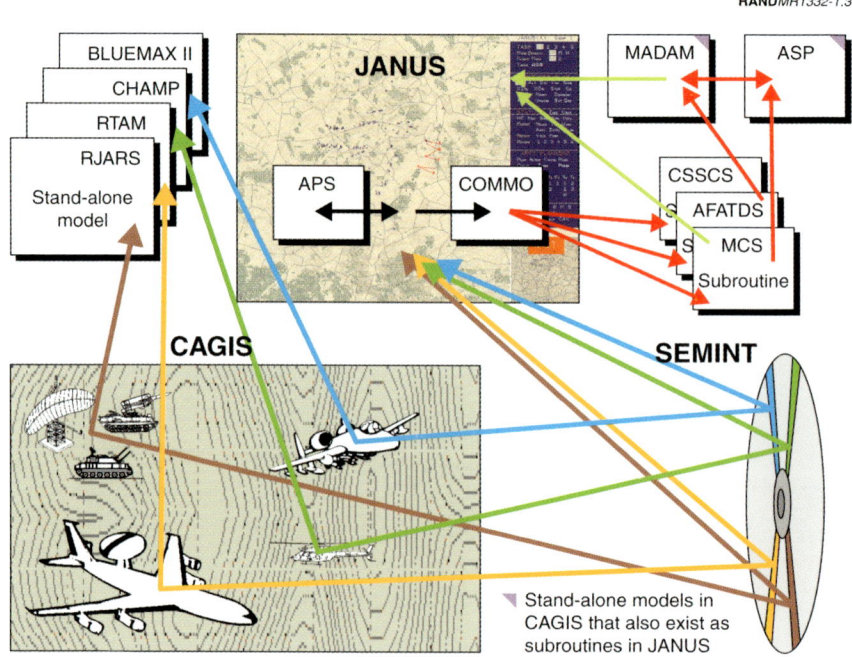

Figure 1.3—High-Resolution Modeling and Simulation Network at RAND

in some cases the delays in decisionmaking involved in the sensor-to-shooter links.

The terrain in the western portion of Kosovo was input to our simulation in a series of steps. The 80×80-kilometer region encompassing the pass and the enemy-occupied region (itself about 40×40 kilometers) were the focus of the work. Overlays in the model include Digital Terrain Elevation Data (DTED) Level II (30-meter spacing) terrain elevation data, foliage data, and feature data such as roads, bridges, and towns.

Some of the concepts and technologies were modeled explicitly, and some had to be represented by parametric effects modeling. Sets of excursions, refined over the course of several iterations, were used to examine each of several sets of options. The results are then used to provide insights on the four research questions postulated earlier.

Chapter Two
HOW MUCH REMOTE "SITUATIONAL UNDERSTANDING" IS ACHIEVABLE IN THE 2015–2020 TIME FRAME?

As mentioned earlier, the first question posed by the ASB asked about the level of intelligence or "situational understanding" a commander would have available if only remote assets—such as satellites, manned aircraft, and high/medium-altitude UAVs—were used and no ground organic assets were employed, assuming such remote assets would significantly improve over the next two decades. Although there are many different definitions for such terms as intelligence gathering, data fusion, situation awareness, information dominance, and situation understanding, our intent in this context is to determine whether the commander has sufficient knowledge of the battlefield situation to carry out his mission with a minimum of friendly and noncombatant casualties. This may require that he have accurate and timely information about his own forces (location, status, and plans), the terrain and environmental conditions, and the enemy force levels, status, location, and intent. He and his subordinate commands can then use this information to project options and plan operations.

What we find in answering this question is that the climate of restriction in future SSCs, such as the Kosovo example used here (minimal friendly casualties, minimal noncombatant casualties, minimal infrastructure damage), makes exhaustive data collection necessary. At the same time, the enemy is expected to make use of cover and concealment in rough terrain and urban areas, to intermingle with noncombatants, and to use deception and decoys. All these factors weigh in, suggesting that data collection itself may be the limiting factor in the next two decades. Thus, we find that the normal sequences of collecting, processing, and fusing data and then arriving at an appraisal of the situation are expected to be stymied. In particular, we find that *the commander will be able to discriminate only a portion of the targets, and many of those will be intermingled with noncombatants.*

The remainder of this chapter examines this finding in more detail, starting by discussing the types of remote assets likely to be available in the proposed time frame and their characteristics and capabilities, and then discussing their limitations when employed in the scenario.

WHAT REMOTE INTELLIGENT CAPABILITIES ARE LIKELY TO BE AVAILABLE IN THE TIME FRAME?

In the time frame considered (2015–2025), an array of different remote sensor types should be available to the BCT force. Figure 2.1 shows illustrations of four such systems: (1) Discoverer II/Starlight; (2) Improved JSTARS (E-8D RTIP); (3) Global Hawk (Tier II+ UAV); and (4) Predator (RQ-IA). Future space-based surveillance systems are exemplified by Discoverer II, a constellation of low-earth-orbit satellites with a typical revisit time of 15 minutes (assuming a 24-satellite set). This system can cover large areas with synthetic aperture radar (SAR) and ground moving target indicator (GMTI) radar.

The Joint Surveillance Target Attack Radar System (JSTARS) is already a very capable system and is scheduled for many improvements over the next decade or so. However, it still has some major impediments in mixed terrain. The system's low operating altitude (36,000–42,000 feet) and long standoff to avoid air defenses (as much as 200 miles) combine to produce low grazing angles, which are problematic for foliage penetration (FOPEN) and result in large areas of masked terrain.

High- and medium-altitude endurance UAVs such as Global Hawk and Predator offer the most promise for reliable FOPEN and detection of targets. Global Hawk, flying at up to 65,000 feet (out of the range of most air defense systems), can overfly the target area with minimal terrain blockage. Predator, flying at 26,000 feet and below, can give a higher-resolution electro-optic (E/O) image of the target set, along with a SAR image.

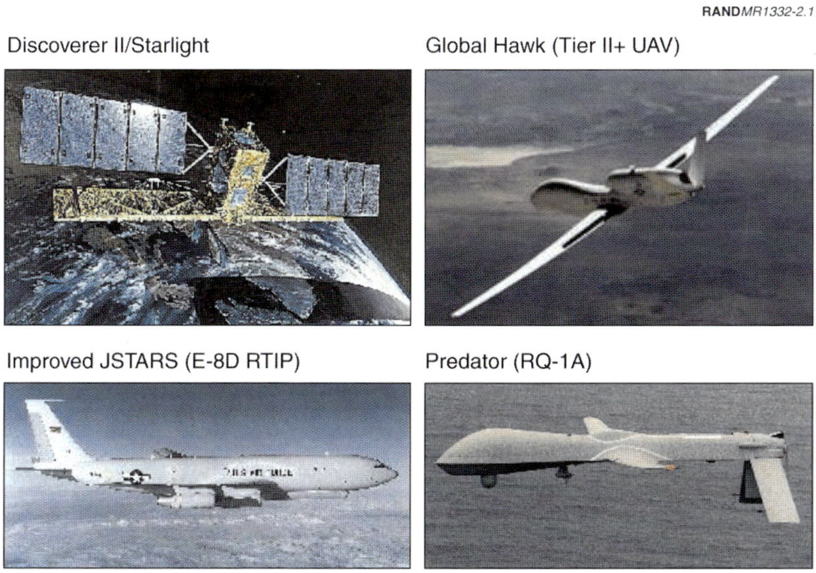

Discoverer II/Starlight   Global Hawk (Tier II+ UAV)

Improved JSTARS (E-8D RTIP)   Predator (RQ-1A)

Figure 2.1—Remote Intelligence Assets Available in the Time Frame

When we look more closely at these four remote platforms in Table 2.1, many shortcomings appear for surveillance of rough, foliated areas. For example, with Discoverer II, the user can achieve resolution in the spot mode down to one foot. Unfortunately, even when transmitting in the X-band, the radar is only moderately suited to FOPEN and will not be able to distinguish vehicle types in most forms of cover.

Upgrades slated for JSTARS include an upgraded SAR and inverse synthetic aperture radar (ISAR) radar, new engines, more powerful signal processing, Link 16 upgrades (allowing it to pass ground tracks to more platforms), and, possibly, automatic target recognition. Unfortunately, low grazing angles occlude most hilly and mountainous areas from sensing because of line-of-sight (LOS) difficulties. Even when targets are in the open, JSTARS can only recognize some unique targets such as tanks and self-propelled howitzers.

Global Hawk and Predator offer advantages of endurance and lookdown angle. Global Hawk has the payload capacity and size to be

Table 2.1
Expected Performance Levels of Remote Assets

System	Altitude	Payload	Coverage Area	Resolution	Discrimination
Discoverer II	Walker orbit; 15-minute revisit	X-band SAR: MTI, FTI	100,000 km/hr	3 m SAR 1 m strip 0.3 m spot	Some ID in open
JSTARS-RTIP	36,000–42,000 ft	SAR: MTI, FTI, ISAR	20,000 km/ mission	6x current, with ISAR, ATR	Tracks vs. wheels to target ID
Global Hawk	65,000 ft	E/O and SAR: FOPEN possible	40,000 sq nm or 1,900 spots/ mission (E/O or IR)	SAR @ 1 m, SRA spot @ 0.3 m, E/O NIIRS > 6.5 IR > 5.5	Some ID in open, detection only in foliage
Predator	26,000 ft	E/O or SAR	800 m swath	SAR 1 ft IPR, E/O NIIRS 7 IR NIIRS 5	E/O target ID

SOURCE: Federation of American Scientists.

able to carry a large-aperture radar tuned to efficient FOPEN frequencies of 200 to 1,000 MHz. Even so, this system is only able to spot large vehicles in the trees, is unable to distinguish APCs, tractors, trucks, or other similar platforms, and can estimate speeds only roughly. The most effective use of the system is to cue other lower-altitude platforms such as Predator to confirm the target identification using E/O sensors, although this will be limited because of cloud cover and air defenses.

HOW MUCH SITUATIONAL UNDERSTANDING CAN THESE REMOTE ASSETS PROVIDE?

Given these characteristics and capabilities, the remote assets should be very useful for spotting targets in open areas. Given enough time, sufficient resolution is available to detect, recognize, and possibly identify vehicle types. However, discrimination between enemy infantry and noncombatants is unlikely from high altitude.

However, such remote assets are likely to be much less effective at finding and identifying targets in foliage. Resolution, which is governed by the long wavelength of FOPEN radar, can only provide a "detection" of vehicles; it cannot recognize or identify them.[1] The highest level of location accuracy, regardless of time, is in the tens of meters.

The best use of the remote assets in areas with foliage may be to provide a baseline for change detection and to cue other assets to possible sightings for confirmation. Prior to hostilities, the area may be surveyed with satellites and UAVs and any changes to the background clutter noted. This will enhance tracking performance if, once strategic warning is received, intelligence assets are deployed in time to cover movement routes from the border. Also, intelligence gathering can be used to template the order of battle to help determine where the enemy is *not*.

---

[1] Detection refers to the formal Johnson criteria definition as determined by the available resolution of the sensor (EO or IR). Recent research at CECOM (communication with Alan Tarbell) indicates that technology improvements in FOPEN allow frequent discrimination of targets in wooded areas, at least when a human interpreter can view the radar image. Location accuracy can probably be below 10 meters with such an airborne system.

What drives the usefulness of such assets in foliated areas is the quality of the information that FOPEN radar can provide. Figure 2.2 provides an example of the quality of information that can be provided by FOPEN radar. This image shows a group of vehicles emplaced in terrain with both open and foliated areas. The figure contains the schematic of actual targets, the aerial photograph, the FOPEN SAR image, and a processed image with nominated targets.

Although targets in the trees are detected, they only show up as "blobs," which generally may indicate the presence of vehicles. As can be inferred from the figure, false alarms are also a likely event. Additionally, the process would not discriminate between civilian and military vehicles, and it would not detect dismounted infantry.

A range of possible levels of situational awareness can be represented in the simulation we used for the analysis (shown in Figure 2.3). The

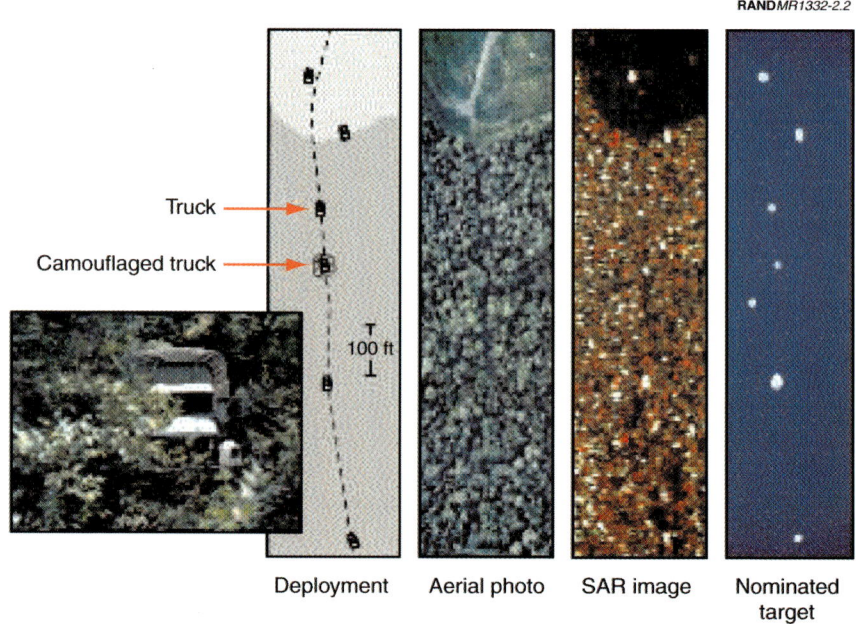

SOURCE: Stanford Research International (SRI). For further information, see Web site at *www.essd.sri.com/penetratingradar/folpen/folpen.html.*

Figure 2.2—Example of Targets Detected Through Foliage

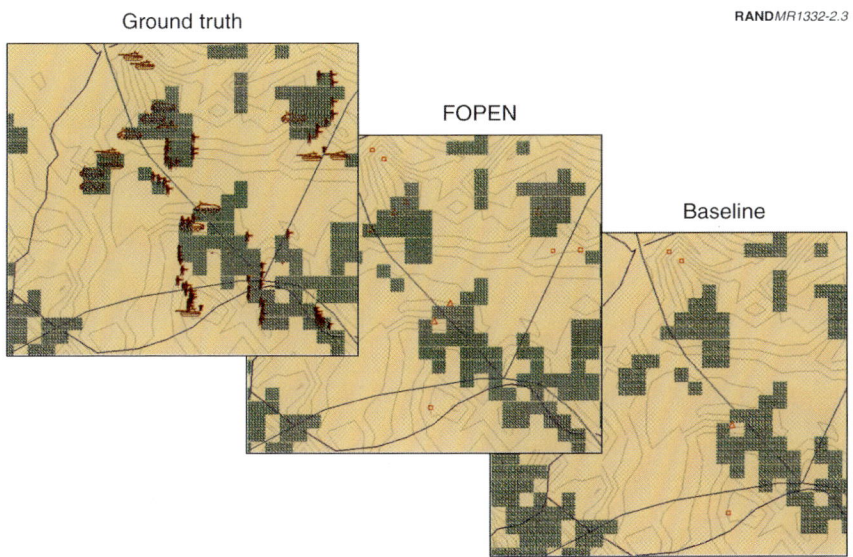

Figure 2.3—Comparison of Current and FOPEN Capabilities Versus Ground Truth

right panel of the figure shows the baseline kind of image that a JSTARS, along with other high-altitude systems that exist today, might be able to provide. Only systems in the open are detected, and those are labeled as tracked or wheeled. The center figure shows the potential added value that sensor technology such as advanced SAR/FOPEN might be able to provide. In this case, there is an ability to acquire targets through trees and an even greater ability to discriminate between tracked and wheeled vehicles. However, these acquisitions are not resolvable into specific target types. The ground truth screen shown on the left details the type and location of every enemy system, whether in the trees or the open.

By comparing the JSTARS or FOPEN image to ground truth, it is evident that the intelligence picture is far from complete. Although noncombatant vehicles and personnel are not shown in this figure, it can be inferred that they would greatly complicate the scene.

To help illustrate the challenge added by the presence of noncombatants, Figure 2.4 shows a scene of a village in Kosovo in 1999. Six

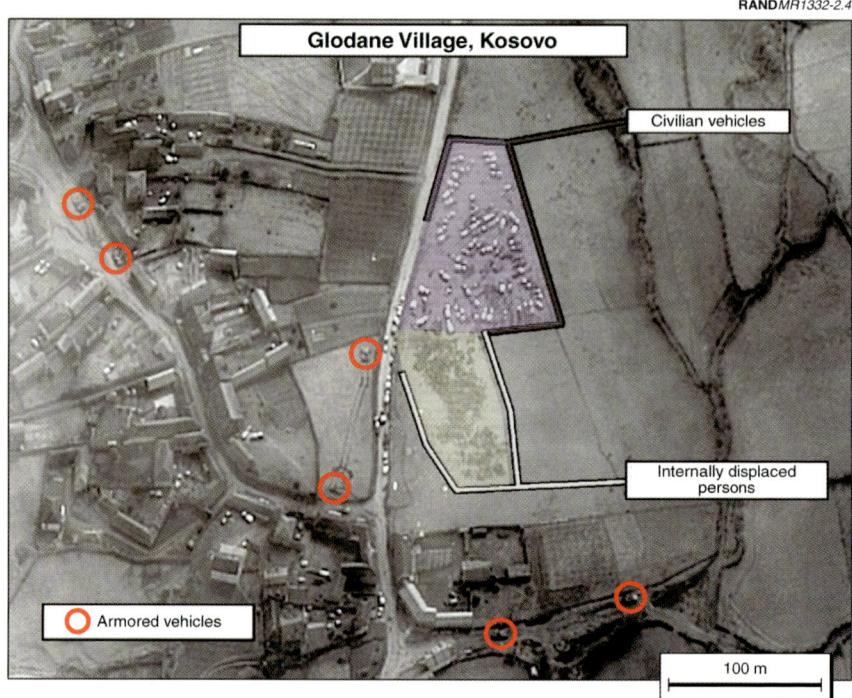

Figure 2.4—Scene of Glodane Village in Kosovo in 1999 Taken by Remote Assets

armored vehicles were acquired by remote assets (indicated by red circles). The enemy vehicles were deliberately placed within the confines of the village, noncombatant (ethnic Albanian) placement was controlled, and the movement of these noncombatants was in high densities along the main roads. The rules of engagement (ROE) in effect at the time required target confirmation before weapons could be released.

Although these vehicles were recognizable as tracked vehicles (in the open), because of their proximity to the civilian population, they could not be attacked without exposing noncombatants to great risk. Even advanced precision-guided weapons were likely to inflict civilian casualties and/or collateral damage to village structures.

As a reference point, in the 1999 Kosovo conflict, even with very strict ROEs, many buildings, vehicles, and individuals were still exposed to weapons released during air strikes, resulting in thousands of noncombatant casualties and collateral damage.[1] In addition to the village of Glodane, shown in the figure, 441 villages were affected by allied force air strikes, resulting in considerable damage. Of those villages affected, 51 percent of the buildings had no damage, while 33 percent had severe damage.

---

[1] According to Human Rights Watch, which documented 3,000–4,000 noncombatant casualties, of which over 500 were fatalities, caused by NATO air strikes. See *http://hrw.org/hrw/reports/2000/nato.*

Chapter Three

WHAT CAN BE ACCOMPLISHED USING A FULL RANGE OF JOINT ASSETS WITHOUT CLOSE COMBAT?

The second question posed by the ASB asked whether the mission can be accomplished without committing ground forces. The excursions employ only long-range fires targeted on the basis of remote and tactical or organic sensor assets. Among the long-range fires systems available in this time frame are air, ground, and naval precision weapons. In addition to the remote assets considered in Chapter Two, we consider some organic assets, which include unmanned ground sensors, advanced fire support systems, and other robotic elements.

What we find in answering this question is that *a reasonable portion of the targets can be located and killed without risking U.S. lives, but a very large number of noncombatants would probably be injured or killed.* Even so, the number of enemy systems killed in the excursion would probably not result in success of the U.S. mission—to evict the in-place battle groups and stop the advancing ones. Given the determination of the enemy, as seen in Operation Allied Force, it is possible that significant losses would not deter them from their objective. Perhaps more important, the historical evidence suggests it is likely that the enemy would have implemented countermeasures to an aggressive U.S. remote application of long-range, standoff fires.

In the rest of this chapter we discuss this finding in more detail, starting with an examination of how the organic and remote sensing assets work together.

HOW DO REMOTE AND TACTICAL (ORGANIC) SENSOR NETWORKS PERFORM?

As noted earlier, many different layers of remote and organic sensors are available to gather targeting information without putting soldiers at risk. Remote assets, such as Discoverer II, JSTARS, and Global Hawk, can spot groupings of targets in the open and, to some extent, in cover. Although their contacts are not sufficient to fire on (and avoid noncombatant losses), they are suitable for cueing other sensing assets for a closer look. The commander's unmanned organic sensing systems—tactical fixed-wing and hovering UAVs—can orbit over the likely target areas and recognize military targets, as well as provide some information about noncombatants in the area. In particular, fast, low-flying tactical UAVs can use E/O sensors to look into woods from different directions and inclinations, while hovering UAVs can attempt to peer horizontally into the woods. The commander can also call for emplacement of acoustic sensors using artillery or helicopter deployment and receive information about moving or idling vehicles—without relying on LOS detection. Of course, the information quality—differentiation of targets, location accuracy, and timeliness—must be appropriate for the specific weapon utilized, and the information provided by the various sensors needs to be fused, the situation assessed, and the targeting decisions made; this remains a critical issue.

Figure 3.1 illustrates some of the organic sensing assets we used to model the tactical targeting capability. For example, we selected the air-deliverable acoustic sensor (ADAS) (36 sensors used in simulation) as the distributed sensor to be used in this scenario because of the relatively hilly terrain, heavy foliage of the environment, and frequently poor weather conditions—all of which limit the use of E/O sensors. Other options (not pictured) that may be available include the improved remotely emplaced battlefield sensor systems (IREMBASS) or the air-delivered Steel Eagle system. Tactical UAVs, such as the fixed-wing Outrider (12 UAVs used in simulation), were used to provide additional targeting information. These were flown at low altitude with paths that would attempt to find targets on reverse-slope locations. A specialized version of a hovering UAV was also included in the analysis; this was represented by the CL-227 (18

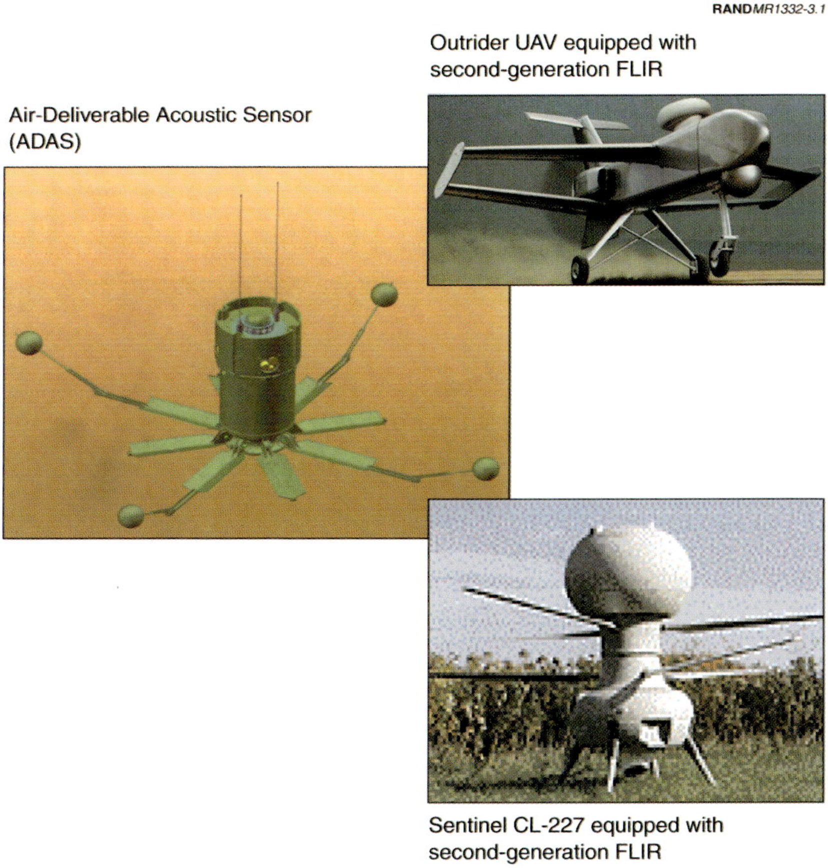

What Can Be Accomplished Using a Full Range of Joint Assets? 23

Air-Deliverable Acoustic Sensor
(ADAS)

Outrider UAV equipped with
second-generation FLIR

Sentinel CL-227 equipped with
second-generation FLIR

Figure 3.1—Examples of Organic Sensing Assets Used

UAVs used in simulation). These were used to peer into tree lines to find difficult-to-detect targets (based on FOPEN cues). We represented both the fixed-wing UAVs and hovering UAVs in the simulation carrying payloads of second-generation stabilized and cooled FLIRs.

With these sensors applied in the context of the scenario, Figure 3.2 shows the unique target acquisitions by sensor type, along with those

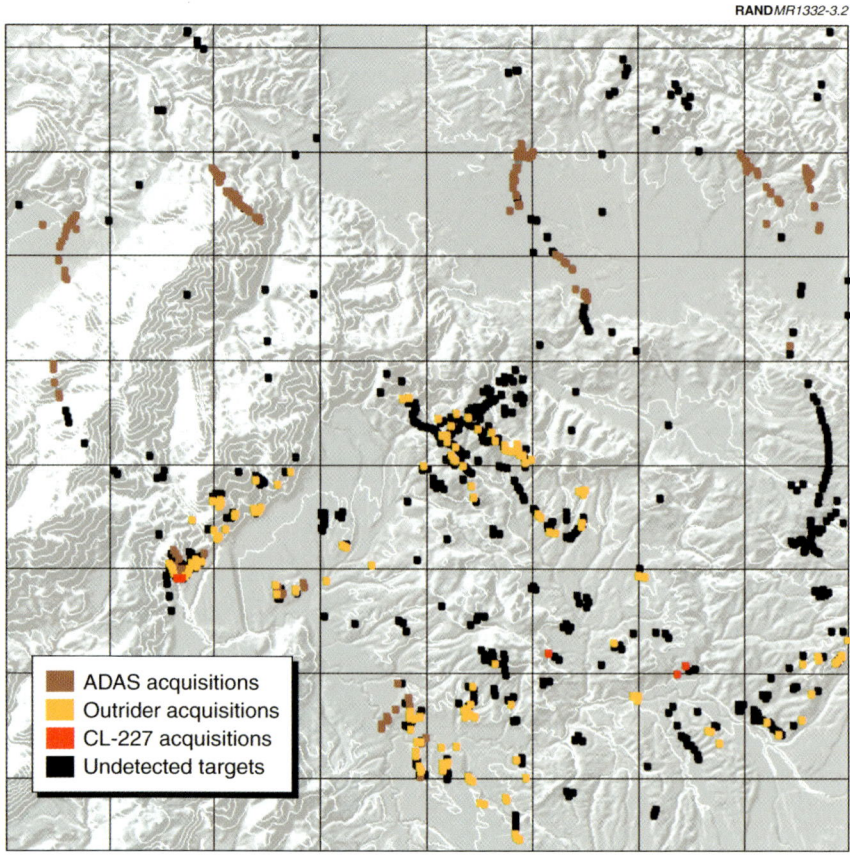

Figure 3.2—Sensor Network Performance

targets that were never acquired.[1] Because the respective sensors have increasing levels of capability and quality of targeting—with the ADAS being the lowest and the hovering UAV being the highest—any target that was acquired by different sensors was credited to the highest-quality system that detected it. Nonetheless, the low-level

---

[1]The standard for acquisition was "recognition" as defined by the Johnson criteria; acquisitions shown in the figure were cumulative over the representative six-hour battle.

ADAS acquisitions were plentiful, more than with any other sensor. These acoustic sensors were placed along the roads and mountain passes—areas in which other sensors would not be likely to survive very long.

The fixed-wing tactical UAV found quite a few targets because of the reverse-slope phenomenology employed by the enemy (hiding behind and firing from a ridge line). The hovering UAV, which was used along tree lines to acquire targets in foliage, ultimately acquired very few. Although it can be argued that such a UAV could be used elsewhere on the battlefield, it would very likely be vulnerable in places that the other sensors were used, given its hovering mode. Altogether, of the 971 targets on the battlefield, about a third (323) were detected by at least one of the systems in the tactical sensor network.

HOW DO LONG-RANGE FIRE SYSTEMS PERFORM?

Given the capabilities of the sensor assets, how do long-range fires perform in the scenario? Rather than develop a detailed targeting plan for the long-range fires, with allocations of fires for each advanced weapon, we opted instead to examine weapon effects parametrically (because of time constraints in the study). In accordance with ASB guidance, we made a series of assumptions. First, we assumed a probability of kill, or P_k, equal to 0.8, regardless of target type or location. In short, we assumed that every target that was acquired could be engaged with a very high degree of success. This kind of reverse-engineering or requirement-based analysis could then be used to help shape the characteristics of weapons needed, determine their number, or ascertain whether weapons can even be developed to meet the requirement.

Second, a kill was assessed on the target that was closest to the "aimpoint" of the target acquisition. This proved to be important with the use of the ADAS, which occasionally miscorrelated targets, triangulating on ghost targets. Stationary target acquisitions (mostly UAV-based) were assumed to be accurate, with the targets found killed and with fusing through foliage assumed possible. Moving-target acquisitions (mostly acoustic sensor-based) were assumed to have low accuracy; unintentional (undetected) targets were engaged, and dead targets were reattacked in many cases.

Third, no secondary kills were permitted (e.g., one kill was allowed per engagement), and target spacing was relatively high.

Given these assumptions, the targeting was relatively straightforward—given a target acquisition, we assumed a P_k equal to 0.8, which was implemented stochastically in the simulation. For stationary targets, this roughly translated to about 260 engagements that resulted in 207 kills. For moving targets, the number of engagements did not match quite so nicely, about 240 engagements producing only 133 kills. Part of the reason for this reduced efficiency is the imprecise nature of acoustic sensors detecting and locating the moving targets. ADAS triangulates multiple sensors to a perceived target. Even with very precise azimuth accuracy, the target closest to the triangulation point was often not the primary target, resulting in either misses or multiple engagements and overkills of the same vehicles. Figure 3.3 shows the effectiveness estimates of the parametric analysis.

In the simulation, targets that were seen were generally killed. In some cases, targets that were not seen were also killed, because of the imperfections in the triangulation process. Overall, total kills were slightly higher than the one-third of targets that were acquired (340 versus 323 out of 971 targets). Figure 3.3 shows the proportions that were moving (133) and stationary (207) and giving some idea of the locations where the targets were killed. It also breaks down the targets killed by type, showing that the 240 kills break down as follows: trucks (121); APCs (103); tanks (38); infantry (36); artillery (29); and air defense (13).

The next step in this evaluation of weapon performance was to examine what kind of weapons might be available to address the stationary targets. (These hidden targets proved to be very difficult to engage in Operation Allied Force in 1999.) Figure 3.4 shows a range of capabilities that advanced technologies might be able to offer in the 2015–2020 time frame.

While FOPEN radar and tactical UAVs might be able to find targets through foliage, the figure shows that current and planned smart munitions are likely to have difficulty reacquiring such targets, given the limited capability of seeker-based sensors (e.g., aperture size and cost). Thus, it was determined that competent munitions, such as

What Can Be Accomplished Using a Full Range of Joint Assets? 27

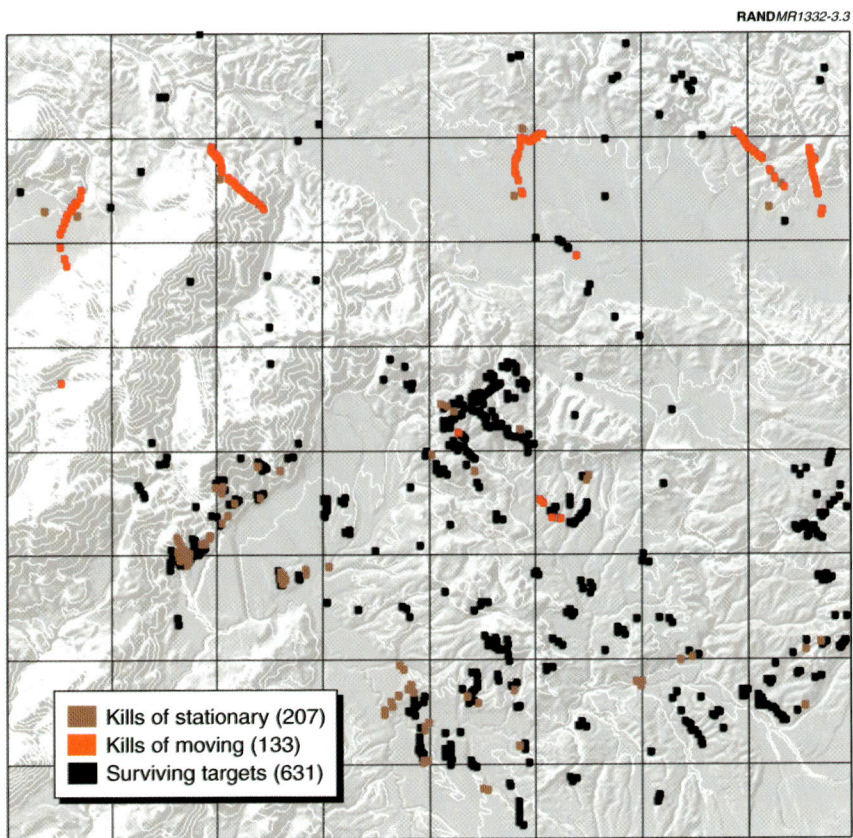

Figure 3.3—Parametric Weapon Performance

guided unitary warhead rockets and small smart bombs, might be able to provide lethality through foliage. The figure shows the rough estimates of such weapons needed to achieve a P_k equal to 0.8. All the weapons shown except for the last case are 250-pound bombs with different delivery accuracies—circular error probables (CEPs)—and target location errors (TLEs); the last case is the standard 2,000-pound Joint Direct Attack Munition (JDAM) with DAMASK under different TLEs. It is evident that without small TLEs, the number of munitions required to achieve one kill is high regardless of CEP.

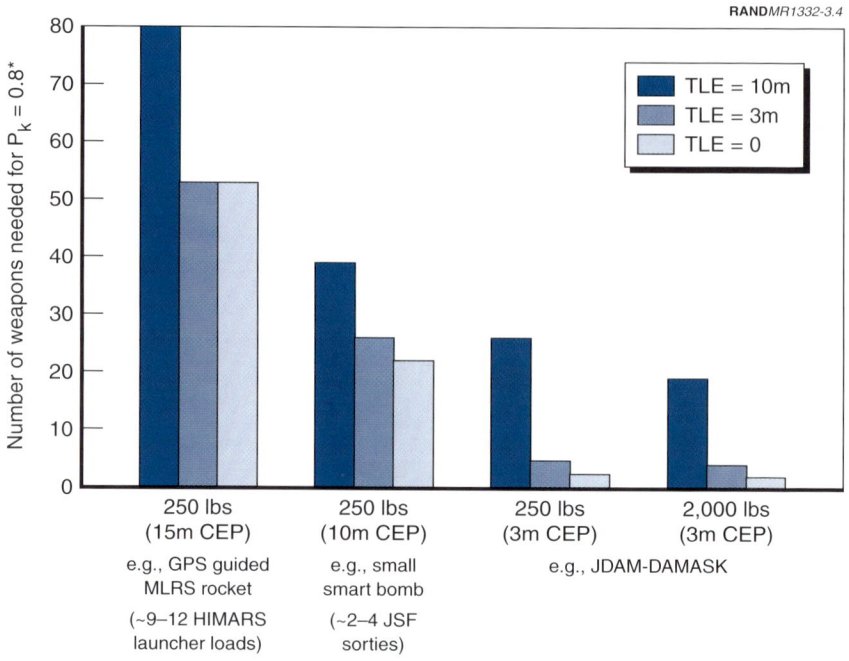

*One hard target (K-Kill) using JMEM methodology.

Figure 3.4—Capabilities of Advanced Technologies Weapons to Kill Stationary Targets

WHAT ARE THE EFFECTS OF LONG-RANGE FIRES ON NONCOMBATANTS?

Given the restrictive ROE, the issue of noncombatants is a serious concern. (The appendix discusses these concerns and our approach to calculating noncombatant casualties.) During the early part of the conflict in Kosovo, the density of population varied throughout the region. We estimate that in densely populated areas, there could be as many as or more than 1,500 noncombatants per square kilometer. This is in contrast to relatively sparser areas (such as in the countryside) where the civilian population density might be as low as 15 per square kilometer. Clearly, these are rough estimates only, primarily used here for evaluating the potential noncombatant problem in this SSC.

An illustration of noncombatant effects is shown in Figure 3.5, which shows the Glodane village addressed earlier in Chapter Two. Assuming a comparatively precise weapon (a modified 250-pound small smart bomb with JDAM-DAMASK and with 3-meter TLE), the figure now shows affected areas when four bombs are dropped against the vehicle in the center of the image. The inner, overlapping circles show the effective area against medium targets, while the outer circle shows the collateral damage area against personnel in the open. Here, the four bombs result in a 36 percent probability of injury

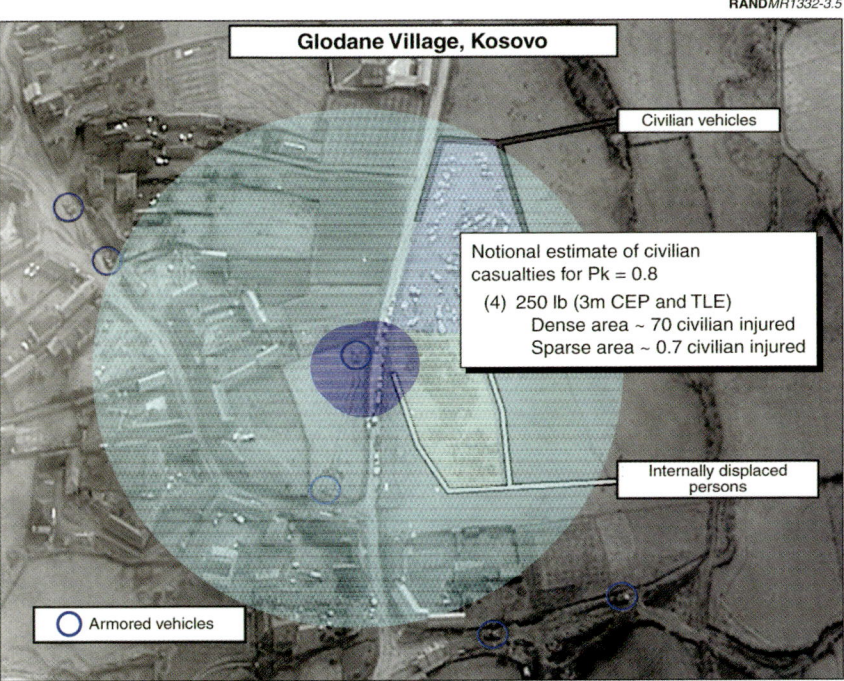

Figure 3.5—Illustration of Noncombatant Effects of Dropping Four 250-Pound JDAM with 3-Meter TLE

within the outer circle. Although the target is the armor vehicle in the center, it is quite apparent that much of the village is within the blast area of the bombs.

Assuming the population density for urban areas described above, we find that a single target engagement can result in as many as 70 casualties (according to our methodology shown in the appendix). Only half as many 2,000-pound bombs (with the same 3-meter accuracy) would be needed to achieve a P_k of 0.8 as the 250-pound bombs, but the casualties are higher.

Aggregating these engagement results over the projected 500 strikes in this long-range fires situation, the casualty expectations are quite high. For stationary targets, we estimate about 260 engagements, assuming no error on target recognition (e.g., every target is real); we assume that 20 percent of the strikes are in "dense" population areas and that 80 percent are in "sparse" areas. We also assume four small smart bombs (the estimate needed to reach the 0.8 P_k) with 3-meter CEP and 3-meter TLE (the most optimistic assumption). Given these assumptions, some 3,500 casualties might be expected. Under less optimistic assumptions, as many as 6,000–7,000 casualties may be expected (see the Appendix). Based on historical data, about 10 percent of these might be expected to be fatalities.

For moving targets, the picture is somewhat better. We estimate about 240 engagements, accounting for acoustic sensor error. Smart submunitions with limited collateral damage are used rather than large unitary warheads, in this case precision-guided munitions (PGMs) like the Low-Cost Autonomous Attack Submunition (LOCAAS) or Damocles, for which one submunition is needed to achieve a P_k equal to 0.8. These smart munitions are assumed to have a very discerning automatic target recognition (ATR) system, which can discriminate between military and nonmilitary vehicles 95 percent of the time. The nonmilitary vehicles that are hit might have several passengers each, with a resulting casualty count of perhaps 50.

For historical comparison, the number of noncombatant casualties attributed to the allied forces in the Kosovo conflict, under strict ROEs, was estimated to be between 3,000 and 4,000, with over 500 confirmed dead (the majority in Kosovo).[1] The presence of so many refugees and internally displaced persons greatly complicated NATO attacks in 1999.

---

[1]According to Human Rights Watch; see *http://hrw.org/hrw/reports/2000/nato*. Of the 500 noncombatant deaths, 300 were in Kosovo.

Chapter Four

DOES ADDING GROUND MANEUVER, POSSIBLY CLOSE COMBAT, WITH THE BCT OFFER ADVANTAGES?

The third research question examined the effectiveness of a rapid-reaction force both in lieu of and in conjunction with the remote firepower previously shown. In this scenario, the brigade-sized ground force is now available to the ground commander. Employing relatively conservative doctrine and TTPs, the brigade enters through mountain passes from Albania, forces its way northwest, clears the roughly 40×40-kilometer area of Serb forces, and blocks any follow-on reinforcements.

When we run the simulation to answer the research question, we find that *with the use of ground forces, the mission is likely to be successful; however, success comes at a relatively high cost.* In some sense, depending on the aggressiveness of the application of standoff fires, U.S. casualties might be spared with increased risk to noncombatants. It is also important to note that the enemy has the advantage in terrain, preparation, and cover, and can effectively ambush the rapid-reaction force.

In the remainder of this chapter we discuss this finding in more detail, starting with an examination of how the future brigade-sized ground force might be structured.

HOW MIGHT A FUTURE BCT BE STRUCTURED, AND HOW WOULD IT BE USED?

Many different variations of BCTs have been proposed, ranging from very light units to ones with integrated engineering, air defense, fire

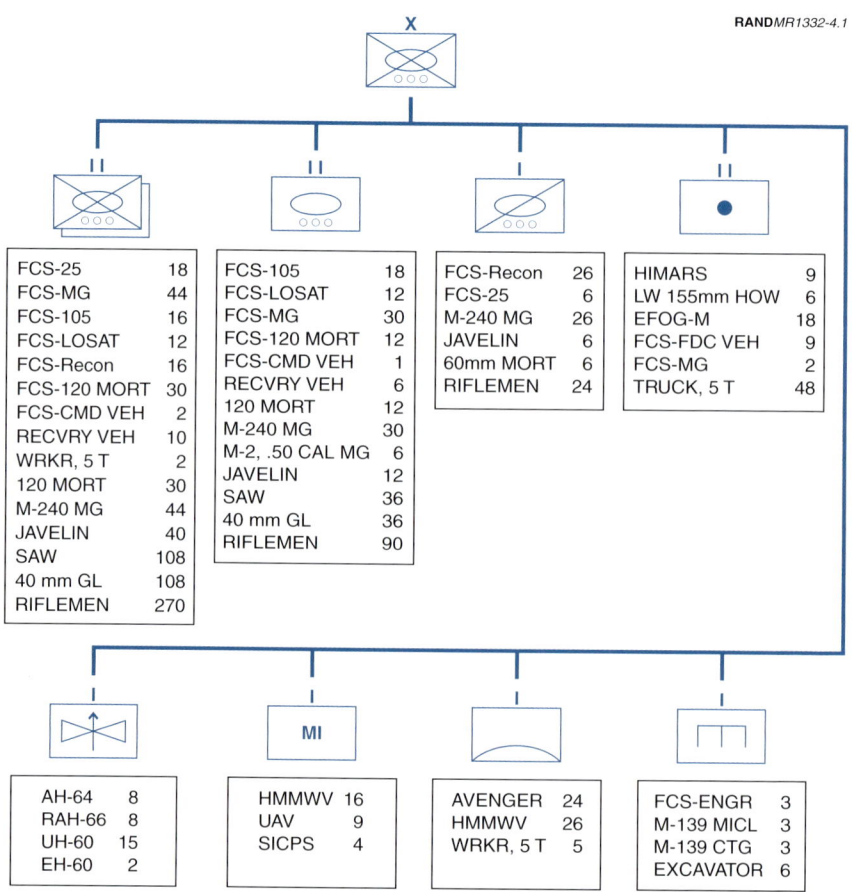

Figure 4.1—Notional BCT Structure Assumed for the ASB Study

support, and aviation. For this study we assumed a three-battalion structure, as shown in Figure 4.1.[1]

---

[1] The organization assumed here is different from the IBCT structure that has been developed by TRADOC. At the time of this writing, capabilities such as aviation and advanced artillery (e.g., High-Mobility Artillery Rocket System, or HIMARS) are not organic to the force. Further discussions with TRADOC representatives have revealed that in this scenario it is unlikely that the IBCT would deploy without such capability, if it were available.

This unit is task-organized and has combined arms capability at a relatively low level, including organic advanced indirect-fire and aviation units. The platforms themselves are primarily variations of 20-ton vehicles with Level III protection.

The first phase of the ground maneuver operation involves moving two battalions from the mountain passes to an initial series of terrain features—a defended set of river crossings (see Figure 4.2) and choke points. After this is accomplished, the second phase of the maneuver requires the battalions to fight their way across wooded areas to clear the in-place Serb battle groups. The operation is led by reconnaissance forces, which probe the Red defenses and engage when fired upon. The lead two battalions are followed by a third, which is envisioned to later effect a passage of lines (to block Red from reinforcing its units).

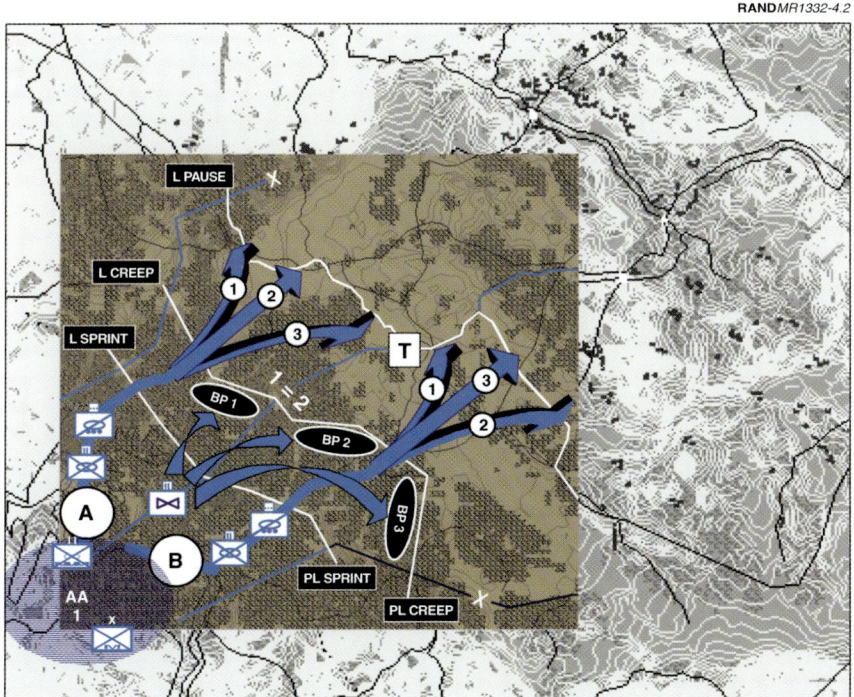

Figure 4.2—Illustration of Baseline Ground Maneuver Operation for BCT

The Red defensive concept, implemented by our designated Red commander, is not new. Many of the actions were carried out using tactics observed during the 1999 Kosovo campaign, while others are standard Russian doctrine. In particular, the Red forces took on the form of battle groups or reinforced companies that employed combined arms tactics. They were positioned in optimum locations at critical tactical positions—bottleneck areas—such as river crossings and hill slopes overlooking movement paths. In most cases, the Red armor was positioned within tree lines while still maintaining good fields of fire (e.g., we assumed that cones of fire were created). Extensive terrain is available for concealment, and preplanning is an advantage for the Red forces. The Red infantry was assumed to be in defilade or dug in, making them a very difficult target to destroy. Resupply uses cover and concealment during movement, and where cover is not available, air defense artillery (ADA) is employed in overwatch. Finally, cannons, mortars, and MRLs are available for fire support.

HOW DOES THE BASELINE FORCE FARE?

With no specialized technology augmentations such as robotic vehicles or APS, the baseline Blue force suffered extensive losses. Figure 4.3 details the kills and losses attributable to each type or class of system in the baseline case, showing that the loss-exchange ratio (LER) was 1.25, calculated given the 136 kills to 109 losses. Fixed-wing aircraft, dropping sensor-fused weapon (SFW) submunitions on moving Red targets, accounted for a moderate number of kills and no losses. Helicopters were less successful against the enemy air defenses and AT-8 missiles. Manned reconnaissance vehicles encountered the most targets and received the most losses (39 percent). BCT direct-fire systems had fewer engagements than the reconnaissance force, and the ancillary systems such as air defense, command and control vehicles, and combat support (AD, C2, and CS, respectively) all sustained losses to enemy artillery and direct fire. In terms of the enemy kills, 60 percent came from T-72S/T-84, with another 20 percent coming from BTR.

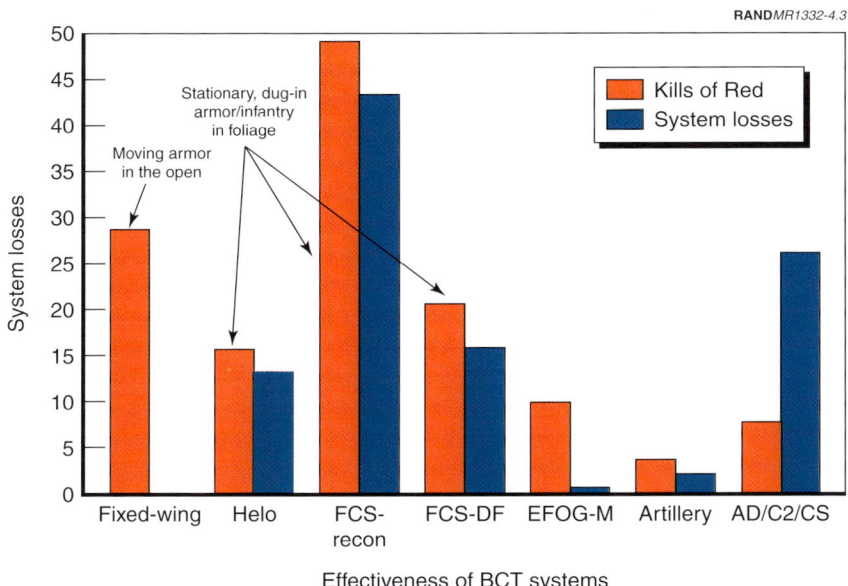

Figure 4.3—Kills and Losses by Type or Class of System in Baseline Case

Figure 4.4a shows the kills of Red systems in the baseline case. Only 136 of the more than 900 enemy systems were attrited, most of them in the tree lines involving direct fire. Indirect fire accounted for a very limited number of kills. The primary reason for this was the presence of foliage, which greatly reduced the effectiveness of the organic precision-guided weapons' sensors. Furthermore, even though the BCT was equipped with superior sensors, because the enemy was positioned in hide locations, it often achieved the first shot during the direct-fire engagements.

As a result of the positional advantage of the enemy forces, Blue forces suffered significant attrition during these direct-fire engagements. Figure 4.4b shows the specific locations of the losses of the BCT's systems. Most of these losses resulted from direct fire in ambushes; however, a combination of mines and overwatching fire, along with indirect fire, proved very effective as well.

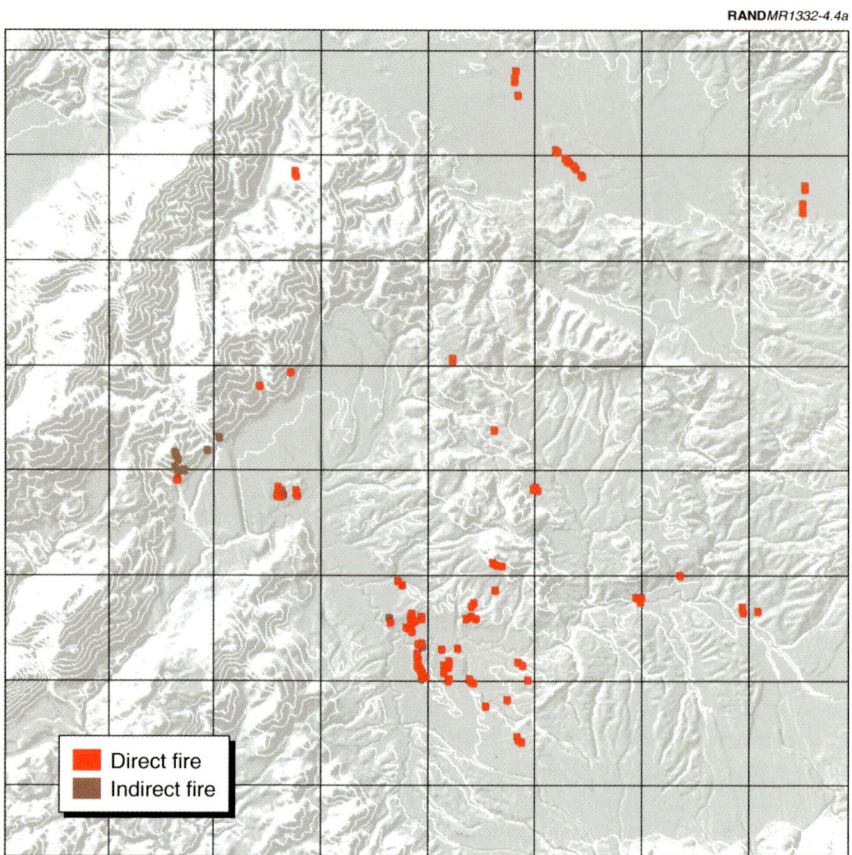

Figure 4.4a—BCT Kills of Red Systems in the Baseline Case

HOW CAN BASELINE PERFORMANCE BE IMPROVED?

To potentially improve the outcome of the baseline case just shown, we considered a range of advanced technologies for the BCT. Among the technologies considered in this study (and illustrated in Figure 4.5), the 20-ton FCS-type manned platforms could integrate robotic vehicles in the reconnaissance unit (one of the most dangerous as-

Does Adding Ground Maneuver with the BCT Offer Advantages? 39

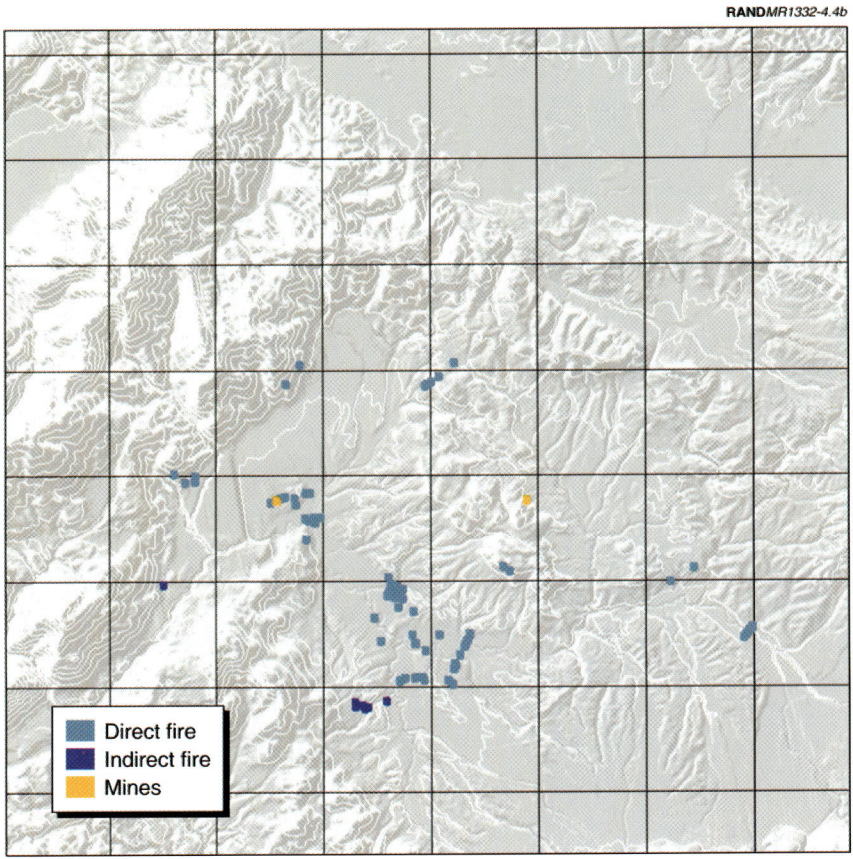

Figure 4.4b—BCT Losses of Blue Systems in the Baseline Case

pects of the mission); mount APS, advanced armor, special crew interfaces, and powerful sensors; and incorporate advanced munitions.

The robotic reconnaissance vehicle assumed in this study is smaller in profile (about 1.5 meters high) and lighter in weight (10 tons) than the manned vehicle. It is also assumed to have a 5-meter mast with second-generation FLIR and high-power optics. The vehicle can also

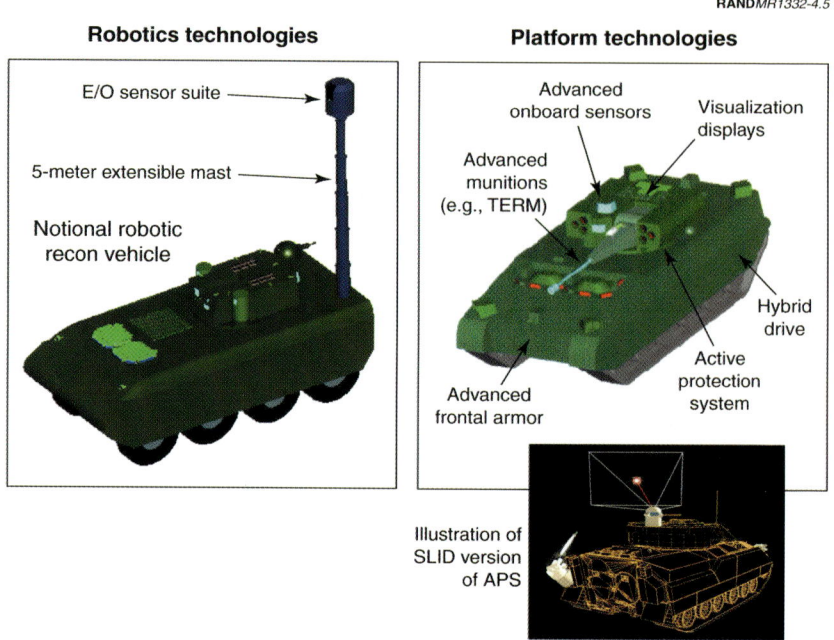

Figure 4.5—Key Technologies Used to Improve BCT Performance

be equipped with a "quickfire" system that senses muzzle flash and immediately returns fire. It can also be equipped with APS similar to the manned vehicles. Each of these technologies and their impact of force effectiveness is examined and discussed in the excursions below.

Table 4.1 summarizes the outcomes of many different technology excursions. The upper row constitutes runs without APS on any of the vehicles. The first cell is the baseline condition, with manned reconnaissance vehicles. It shows the loss-exchange ratio (LER) achieved (1.25, as discussed above) and shows the Red losses (136) and Blue losses (109) that are the basis of the LER calculation. The next cell has unarmed robotic vehicles replacing the manned FCS reconnaissance vehicles. These are somewhat smaller and lighter (10 tons) than the FCS vehicles, and their loss (21 were killed, as shown in parentheses) is not counted in the LER. When armed with an ideal-

Table 4.1

Outcomes of Different Technology Excursions

	Baseline Manned BCT	BCT with Unarmed Robot Recon	BCT with Armed Robot Recon[b]	BCT with Quickdraw[c]	BCT with Long-Range Fires and Quickdraw[d]
No APS	LER=1.25 Losses: 136/109	LER=1.30 Losses: 129/99 (+21)	LER=1.61 Losses: 135/84 (+18)	LER=1.76 Losses: 143/81 (+16)	LER=4.04 Losses: 218/54 (+5)[e] (+noncomb.)
APS[a]	LER=1.59 Losses: 140/88	LER=1.73 Losses: 133/77 (+19)	LER=1.79 Losses: 138/77 (+14)	LER=2.45 Losses: 147/60 (+10)	LER=4.87 Losses: 224/46 (+3) (+noncomb.)

[a] Small Low Cost Interceptor Device (SLID)–like APS with the following characteristics: single launcher, 12 shots, probability of effectiveness = 0.9, hardness = 0.9, with one-second recovery rate (assumed to be ineffective against 125mm KEP rounds).

[b] Armed robotic reconnaissance vehicle equipped with four notional LOS anti-tank missiles and machine gun.

[c] Quickdraw involves a robotic reconnaissance vehicle with muzzle-flash detection, immediate return fire, four Javelin, and machine gun.

[d] Long-range fires involve a two-hour application of remote fires; with earlier methodology this would result in about 1,400 noncombatant casualties.

[e] Numbers in parentheses indicate robotic reconnaissance vehicle losses. Because they were unmanned, these systems were not counted in the LER.

ized mini-LOSAT missile,[1] the robotic reconnaissance system equipped force achieves a 1.61 LER, through increased kills and reduced losses. Adding "quickdraw," which represents an automated fire-control system, to the robotic reconnaissance vehicles further improves the LER to 1.76. The most dramatic effect is achieved when a two-hour, long-range-fire attack using a combination of long-range fires precedes the ground battle. These deep fires are expected to produce 131 kills but, using the assumptions and methodology described earlier, could result in 1,400 noncombatant casualties.[2]

---

[1] No minimum range is required for the LOSAT missile to engage.

[2] The purely ground-based cases shown in the table (the first four columns) have some noncombatant losses. However, because of very tight rules of engagement and combined precision-guided weapons, there are few noncombatant losses during engagements.

The second row shows the same condition, but with APS added to all the fighting vehicles. This resulted in improved survivability and somewhat better lethality. The best that could be achieved with this ground maneuver option was an LER of almost 5.

We examined in more detail how APS and quickdraw helped the BCT fight, particularly in rapid direct-fire exchanges. In one run, the robotic reconnaissance force had 18 of its 24 systems fired on (75 percent), and in 11 instances the APS protected them. In all but one case (90 percent), the reconnaissance vehicles fired back after the APS activated. As noted in the table, we did not assume that the APS system could effectively protect against kinetic energy (KE) rounds. This assumption appears supportable in this scenario, because the average kill by a KE round was found to be just over 800 meters. The 1999 ASB report estimated that detection, location, launch, and deflection of a KE round was not likely at this range.

Quickdraw similarly helped the reconnaissance force survive by quickly firing back when a flash was detected, which helped the APS system to be less overwhelmed. However, there were some anomalies in the engagements, because the system sometimes would shift engagement priority from an already targeted enemy vehicle to another that just fired. More research is required to determine optimum targeting logic, especially since robotic vehicles, in this study, were assumed to be relatively expendable (e.g., not included in the LER).

The best LER for the ground maneuver options was achieved when all improvements were in place: long-range fires, armed robotic reconnaissance vehicles, APS, and quickdraw. A breakdown of system contribution for this case in shown in Figure 4.6, which is the counterpart of Figure 4.3. (The long-range fires engagements that resulted in 131 kills are not shown in this figure.) As noted in Table 4.1, the LER for this case was nearly 5 (4.87), with 224 kills to 46 losses. Here, Blue fixed-wing aircraft made less of a contribution than in the baseline case, because fewer surviving targets presented themselves. This was attributed to a relatively successful long-range fires attack. Blue helicopters engaged less often and survived more than in the baseline case, and the Blue reconnaissance and direct-fire elements had more effective exchanges. However, losses of the AD, C2, and CS systems were still somewhat problematic. All told,

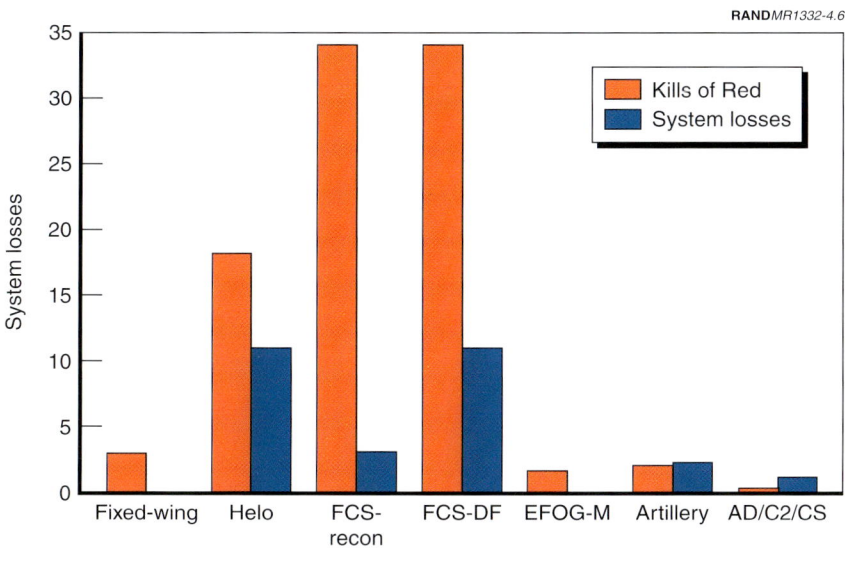

Figure 4.6—Kills and Losses by Type or Class of System in the Best Performance Case

long-range fires attrited 131 of the 224 Red systems, and the majority of the FCS engagements are with dismounted infantry. On the Red side, T-72S/T-84 achieved 30 percent of the kills and the BTR achieved 39 percent.

Figure 4.7 shows the attrition outcome of the best performance BCT case. The 131 kills achieved by long-range fires shows up strongly on the image (shown in dark red). These effects are located both in the enemy reinforcing units in the north and the defensive enemy units hidden in the woods in the south. As a result of this Red attrition, the BCT was better able to cope with the degraded Red force. The attrition produced by the BCT is also shown in the image (shown in light red). Because of the lethality produced by the long-range fires and the technology improvements to the BCT itself, the BCT suffered many fewer losses than in the baseline case (shown in blue). Most of these losses came from direct-fire engagements.

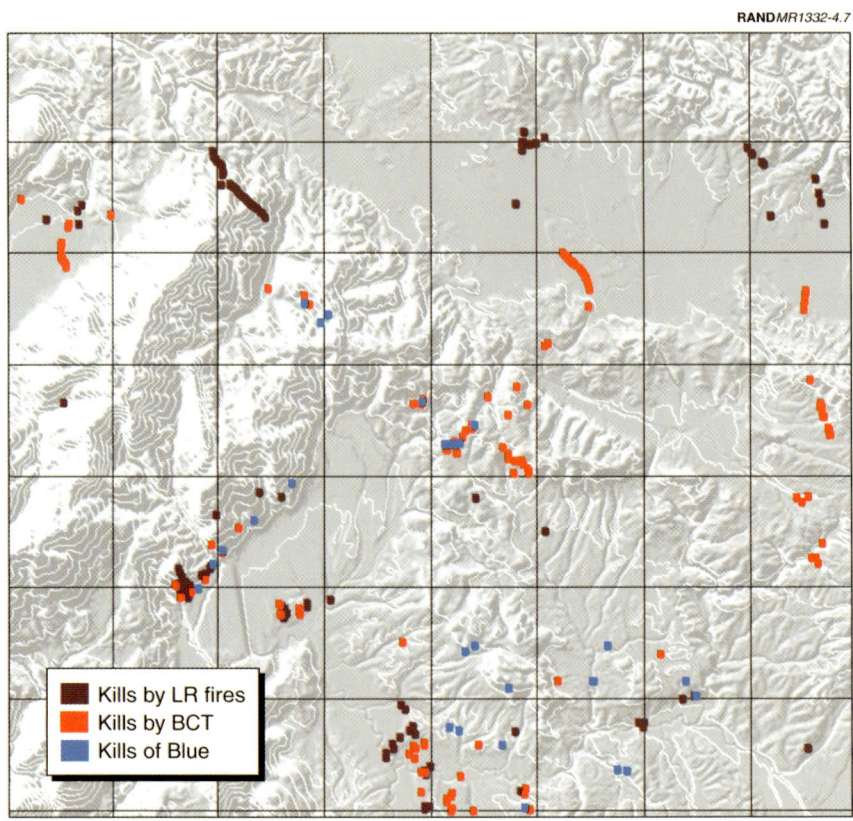

Figure 4.7—Red and Blue Attrition for Improved BCT Case

OBSERVATIONS ON THE USE OF GROUND FORCES

Although different tactics and technologies were seen to provide dramatic improvements in force performance as measured by the LER, it is worthwhile to emphasize that the use of ground forces in general allowed the fundamental mission to be achieved. Unlike in the remote-fires case, where the enemy can opt to flow in more forces as some portion are attrited en route, the use of ground forces tends to decisively counteract this flow. That is, although losses are taken in getting to its position objectives, ultimately the Blue force arrives intact.

Once in place, north of the stationary enemy forces, the Blue force shifts to a hasty defensive position and takes on the encroaching enemy forces with positional (defense) advantage. The reserve Blue battalion can then be used to stabilize the situation and eventually evict the "cut off" enemy forces to the south. Although the follow-on engagement was not addressed in total here, based on earlier research and the nature of the organic weapons within the Blue force, we can conclude that this enemy is not likely to be able to defeat the stationary Blue force.

Chapter Five

WHAT ARE THE IMPLICATIONS OF ENHANCED AIR INSERTION OF THE BCT, SUCH AS BY VERTICAL ENVELOPMENT?

The final research question concerns the use of air insertion of most of the Blue force into blocking positions in the north. This aggressive action changes the fight from a more traditional ground maneuver into a nonlinear engagement, with the Blue force threatening the enemy from different positions. In fact, we found that *the insertion, if successfully accomplished, transforms the basic mission from one that is strictly offensive in nature to one that is predominantly defensive.* This phenomenon occurs because the added mobility provided by vertical insertion gives the BCT the ability to maneuver to operationally significant positions on the battlefield by allowing them to select terrain and exploit intelligence. This kind of expediency results from the BCT getting into position first, possibly creating a defensive position, before the enemy can arrive. This, in turn, results in a much more favorable outcome.

We discuss this finding in more detail in this chapter, starting with a discussion of the airlifter needed to accomplish the mission and a discussion of the mission itself. In the analysis, we assume that the enemy air defenses can be suppressed and that the air insertion is successful. We conclude with an analysis of aircraft survivability for the mission. The reason the research was conducted in this order was to evaluate the potential (theoretically inherent) payoff of vertical envelopment capability. Presuming that there will be a benefit, we then explore the feasibility of such a concept against a modern air defense network.[1]

---

[1]Previous analysis suggests that large aircraft will be extremely vulnerable to a sophisticated air defense network, even at relatively low altitudes. One option may be

48   Exploring Technologies for the Future Combat Systems Program

WHAT WOULD THE AIRLIFTER LOOK LIKE?

The key to flexible air insertion of the force with its less-than-20-ton vehicles may be some form of Future Transport Rotorcraft (FTR). This 20-ton-payload airlifter can carry one or more vehicles, overfly the enemy forces, and drop off the force in unprepared landing areas. A notional image of one of the FTR concepts is shown in Figure 5.1.

WHAT IS THE VERTICAL ENVELOPMENT MISSION?

Interaction with various ASB members and a survey of Kosovo terrain yielded the several potential landing zones for each of three reinforced companies (shown in the screen shot in Figure 5.2 as LZ 1, LZ 2, and LZ 3). Landing zone 1 is in neutral territory on the border of Kosovo and Montenegro, while the other two are in occupied enemy territory and will involve considerable overflight of enemy forces for insertion.

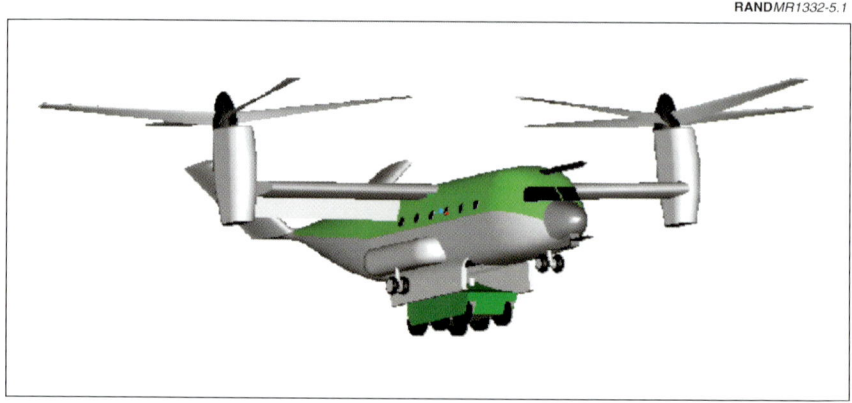

Figure 5.1—Notional Image of One FTR Concept

---

to ingress at high altitude with Joint Suppression of Enemy Air Defenses (JSEAD) and then hover down into a secured (by airborne forces) landing zone.

What Are the Implications of Enhanced Air Insertion of the BCT? 49

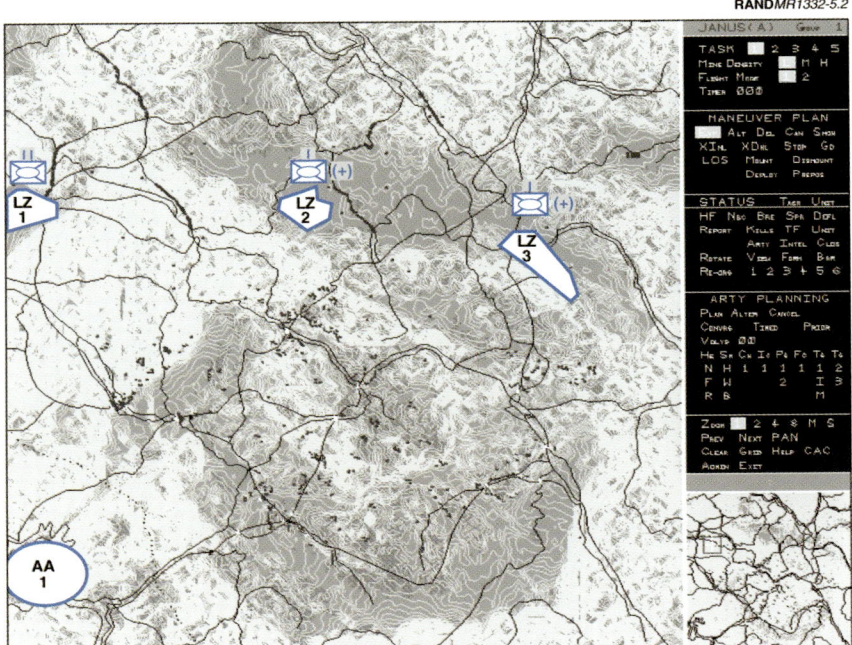

Figure 5.2—Three Potential Landing Zones for the
Vertical Envelopment Mission

The intent of the vertical envelopment mission is to emplace components of the BCT (organized into companies) into position before Red can reinforce the area in the north with the seven battle groups, thus creating a resupply link to the units to the south. Although there are some enemy forces already present in Kosovo (four BGs as before), their concentrations are located mostly in the south to defend against Blue forces entering by ground, where one battalion has already landed at assembly area (AA) 1.

Once the BCT forces are deployed into the landing zones from the air insertion mission, assuming perfect survivability, they move into blocking positions in the north (as shown by the arrows in Figure 5.3). The BCT battalion in the south moves up to engage the stationary, dug-in forces in the south, as before. The advantage for the BCT

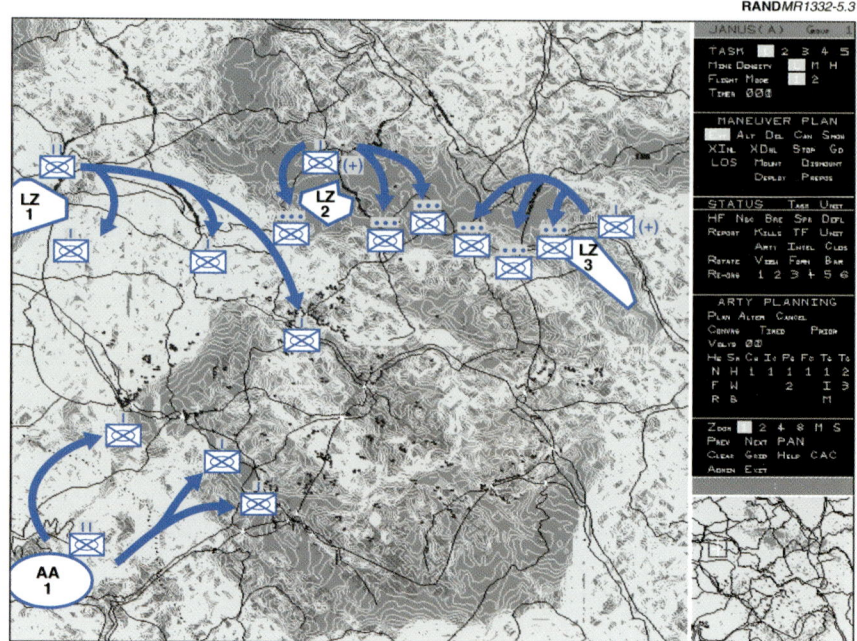

Figure 5.3—Associated Group Maneuver of BCT Units in
Force Envelopment Mission

units in the north, provided they can get into position quickly enough, is that Red can now be engaged and attacked from multiple directions and locations as it advances into the region. As mentioned before, this dramatic improvement in operational mobility shifts the basic nature of the BCT engagement into a more defensive rather than offensive operation. This makes the advancing Red force extremely vulnerable, since the BCT can leverage its superior sensors and weapons. As a result, the enemy can no longer rely on its reinforcements arriving.

We assume that for this air insertion to work, there are no enemy forces in the immediate area of the landing zones. In practical terms, this means that the force lands without a "hot LZ" situation. This could be accomplished either by heavy suppressive fires in the vicinity of the landing zone to neutralize any enemy forces in the area (with possible limitations because of the ROE) or by a preemptive clearing by airborne forces such as the 82nd DRB. In either case, the assumption is rather optimistic. Once deployed, the units are assumed to move out immediately into battlefield positions. Logistics and combat support aspects are assumed to have been resolved.

WHAT ARE THE RESULTS OF THE VERTICAL ENVELOPMENT MISSION?

With the aforementioned assumptions, dramatic improvements in lethality and survivability can be seen with vertical envelopment using FTR air insertion. Table 5.1 (built off Table 4.1) shows that without the benefit of an extensive long-range fires attack (and the associated noncombatant casualties), the LER jumps from around 1.8 to 7.9. This result is generally achieved through reduced numbers of losses of the BCT, since it now fights a predominantly defensive battle. When long-range fires are added, the LER increases even more, from 4.87 in the original case to 13.3. Here, the additional attrition of the enemy improves the lethality of the Blue force by almost 40 percent.

As a result of this improved lethality, fewer enemy systems remain during the direct-fire battle. The BCT is better able to engage the remaining force, effectively improving its lethality and further reducing its losses (both manned and robotic systems).

Figure 5.4 shows the breakdown of the best FTR case with vertical envelopment (the 13.3 LER discussed above). Here, the distribution of kills and losses becomes very different from the baseline case and the "high-tech" ground maneuver cases shown earlier. Now, the long-range fires and FCS direct-fire systems achieve the majority of the kills against the enemy. While attack helicopters, robotic vehicles, and organic artillery systems still participate in the battle, their contribution is much lower overall. This effect can largely be attributed to the shift in the mission, from offense to defense. As the enemy force attempts to move south, it becomes more vulnerable to the BCT, which now has sensor, weapon, and signature advantages.

Also, as can be seen from the figure, the BCT suffered relatively few losses overall, especially the ancillary systems. The unmanned reconnaissance vehicles took 10 percent of the Blue losses. In this

Table 5.1
Outcomes of Flexible Air Insertion, Assuming 100 Percent Survivability

	Baseline Manned BCT	BCT with Unarmed Robot Recon	BCT With Armed Robot Recon[b]	BCT with Quickdraw[c]	BCT with Long-Range Fires and Quickdraw[d]
No APS	LER=1.25 Losses: 136/109	LER=1.30 Losses: 129/99 (+21)	LER=1.61 Losses: 135/84 (+18)	LER=1.76 Losses: 143/81 (+16)	LER=4.04 Losses: 218/54 (+5) (+noncomb.)
APS[a]	LER=1.59 Losses: 140/88	LER=1.73 Losses: 133/77 (+19)	LER=1.79 Losses: 138/77 (+14) LER=7.9 Losses: 237/30 (+12)	LER=2.45 Losses: 147/60 (+10)	LER=4.87 Losses: 224/46 (+3) (+noncomb.) LER=13.3 Losses: 333/25 (+2) (+noncomb.)

[a]SLID-like APS with the following characteristics: single launcher, 12 shots, probability of error = 0.9, hardness = 0.9, with one-second recovery rate (assumed to be ineffective against 125mm KEP rounds).

[b]Armed robotic reconnaissance vehicle equipped with four notional LOS anti-tank missiles and machine gun.

[c]Quickdraw involves robotic reconnaissance vehicle with muzzle-flash detection, immediate return fire, four Javelin, and machine gun.

[d]Long-range fires involve a two-hour application of remote fires; with earlier methodology this would result in about 1,400 noncombatant casualties.

case, the BCT not only accomplishes its mission, but it does so with very few losses (25 manned systems) overall. It is likely that with different force ratios and different tactics, these losses can be reduced even further. For example, because attack helicopters took a fair percentage of total losses, fewer missions overall may be needed, which might place greater emphasis on the BCT weapons. Essentially, different options are available for optimizing the battle.

Continuing the analysis of the best FTR case, Figure 5.5 depicts the locations of the Red and Blue systems killed in the battle from one representative JANUS run. As can be seen from the Red icons (dark

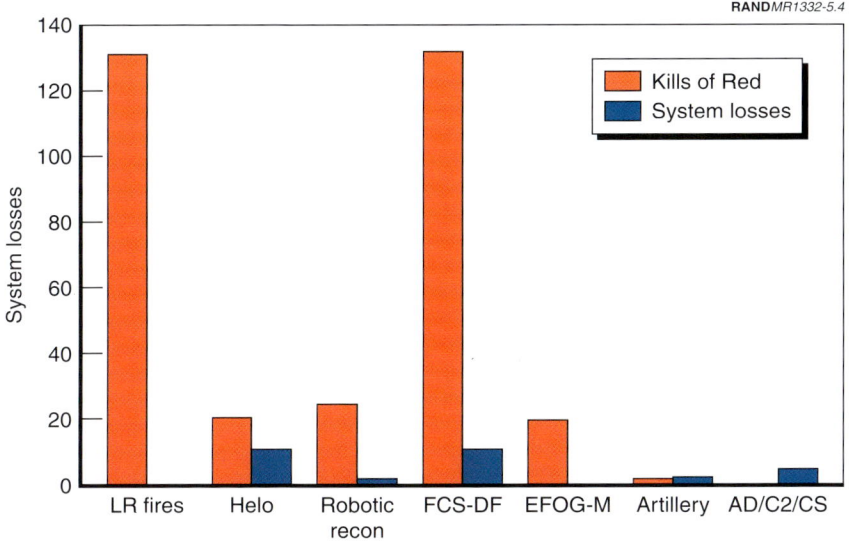

Figure 5.4—Kills and Losses by System for Best FTR Case with
Vertical Envelopment

and light red), enemy attrition is now spread over the screen and is fairly evenly split between the long-range fires and BCT actions. The blue icons representing Blue losses are also fairly spread out. Nonetheless, most of these losses come from the battalion that attacked from ground in the south.

HOW SURVIVABLE IS THE FTR IN THE VERTICAL ENVELOPMENT MISSION?

One caveat to the air insertion case is the assumed survivability of the FTR, both in ingress and in egress. In our initial assumptions, we attributed to the enemy forces two different tracked, mobile air defense systems, the SA-15 and 2S6, which are pictured in Figure 5.6.

The SA-15 is an extremely mobile short-range air defense artillery (ADA) system. Its Doppler radar is effective out to 25 kilometers, and

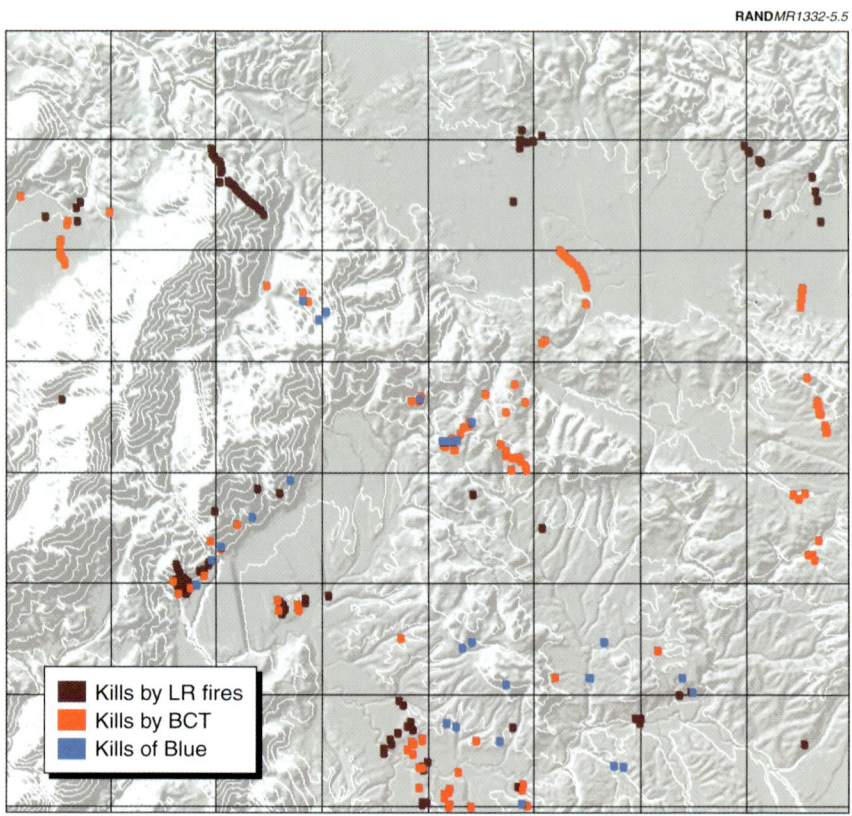

Figure 5.5—Location of Red and Blue Attrition in the
Vertical Envelopment Mission

it can engage targets up to roughly 6,000 meters. The 2S6 is also a highly mobile ADA system that has both guided missiles (SA-19s) and 30-millimeter guns (four barrels). Both guns and missiles are guided by a radar mounted on the top of the ADA unit. The SA-19s have a range of 5 to 8 kilometers. Since both the SA-15 and the 2S6 rely on radar for target engagement, it is possible that an aggressive suppression of enemy air defenses (SEAD) campaign can be waged against them. However, it is possible that such systems can still challenge the FTR operating in enemy-controlled airspace because of

What Are the Implications of Enhanced Air Insertion of the BCT? 55

SA-15 mobile air defense

2S6 tracked air defense unit equipped with 4 (30mm) guns and SA-19 missiles

Figure 5.6—The SA-15 and 2S6 Systems

possible countermeasures, such as blinking or holding radars quiescent until engagement.

Passive, short-range ADA systems may pose an even greater danger to the FTR than the previously discussed radar systems. In this scenario, we assumed that both man-portable air defenses (MANPADS) and anti-aircraft artillery (AAA) are included in the suite of enemy AD systems, the two of which are pictured in Figure 5.7. MANPADS is effective against targets up to 3,500 meters and has a missile range of 0.5 to 5.2 kilometers, while the AAA is a 30-millimeter gun with an engagement range of 3 to 4 kilometers.

Of critical concern is the ability of these systems to operate in the nonemitting mode, that is, using passive thermal or optical sensors. This would make them very hard to find and neutralize until after they have engaged an aircraft. And between small arms fire and tank rounds, these systems represent the next limiting ADA case when RF systems have been suppressed. Special infrared and optical countermeasures may have to be developed to successfully neutralize these systems or their effects on the battlefield.

The coverage of both the longer-range radar systems (SA-15 and 2S6) and shorter-range MANPADS (SA-14/18) and AAA guns is shown in

SA-14/18 man-portable air defense system (MANPADS)
Anti-aircraft artillery (AAA)

Figure 5.7—The SA-14/18 MANPADS and AAA Systems

Figure 5.8. Even though the terrain in Kosovo is quite hilly, it is apparent that the overall coverage is quite good, assuming the numbers of ADA units of each type. Even if intelligence could provide detailed information on the location of the ADA units, very few open paths can be found to emplace the BCT into the two landing zones in enemy territory. Suppression of the radar systems greatly reduces the overall coverage, but again it would be unlikely that very much airspace would be left open, especially against a threat that is familiar with FTR capability and operations.

Using RJARS, we examined several options for the air insertion over what is a relatively sophisticated (though not integrated) air defense site. The large-signature aircraft must overfly radar, IR, and visual systems to reach landing zones 2 and 3. The simulation flew nine FTRs at low altitude from bases in Montenegro to LZs 2 and 3. Two hundred runs of each excursion were made for statistical reliability. Without suppression of the radar-guided sites, all nine aircraft were shot down in the first few minutes. With suppression of the SA-15s and 2S6s, the primary killers were MANPADS, with typically five of the nine aircraft getting through to both landing zones.

It is possible that new protection capabilities similar to the APS for combat vehicles can be created to defend against air defense mis-

What Are the Implications of Enhanced Air Insertion of the BCT? 57

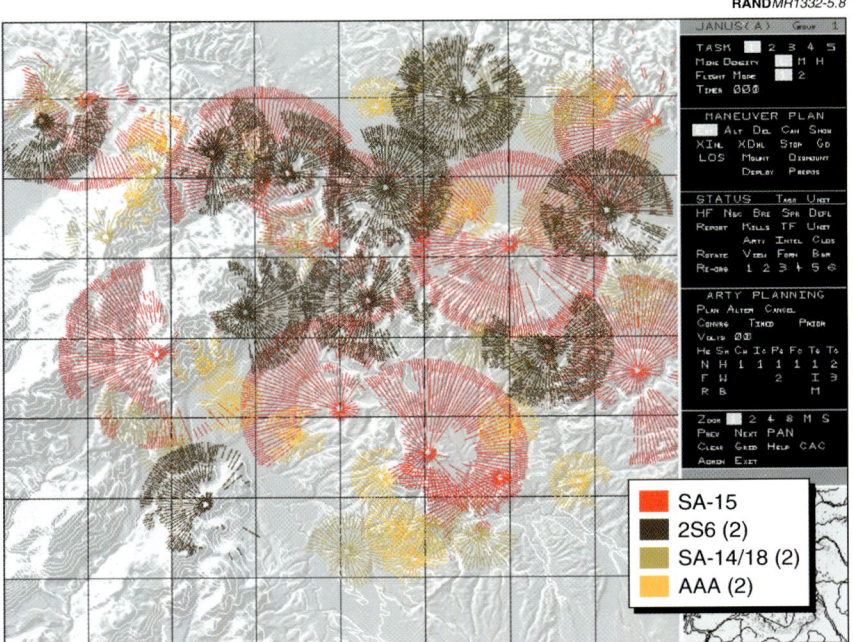

Figure 5.8—Representation of Air Defense Coverage

siles. Various electronic and active countermeasures may increase aircraft survivability. More analysis is needed in this area to validate that the FTR can be sufficiently survivable.

One alternative to the risky air insertion over enemy defenses is to air-deploy only to the first LZ, located in neutral territory. The force can then maneuver over the ground to the previously identified blocking positions. While this operation may require more time to fight through to the other areas than a vertical envelopment with air insertion, it may ultimately prove to be more feasible. However, without the speed associated with the air maneuver, it is possible that the enemy may have enough time to set up in defense. Figure 5.9 shows one possible ground maneuver operation into the same battle positions.

58 Exploring Technologies for the Future Combat Systems Program

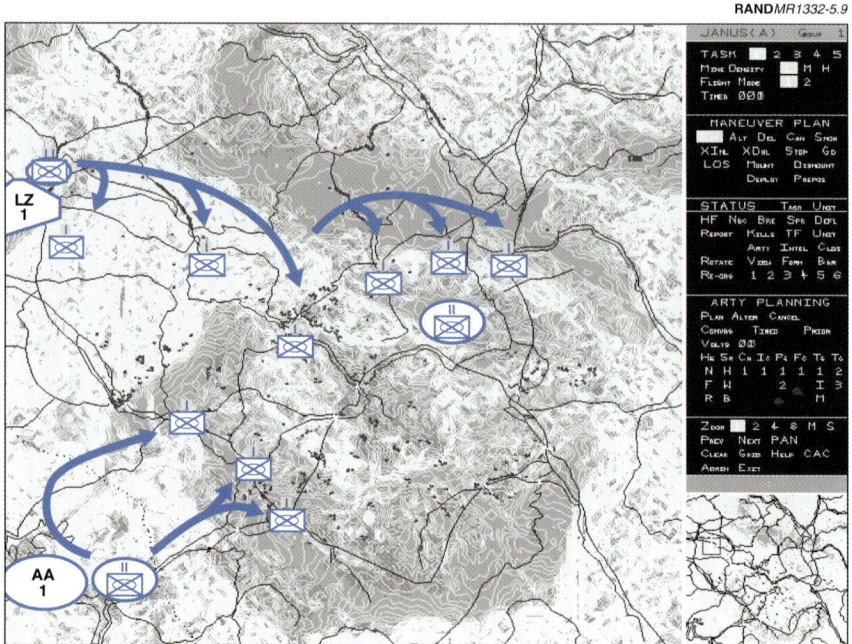

Figure 5.9—Possible Alternative to Vertical Envelopment but Still Using Ground Maneuver

Chapter Six
CONCLUSIONS

This chapter summarizes our key observations, discusses possible enemy countermeasures, and presents some conclusions and recommendations.

KEY OBSERVATIONS

In summary, we found that an enemy who relies on cover, concealment, deception, intermingling, and dispersion will be difficult if not impossible to monitor from overhead assets (even in the 2015–2020 time frame of the analysis). Additionally, by our assessment, organic ground sensors and overhead assets show much promise in finding enemy assets (in the open); precision firepower can provide attrition, but the mission of ousting or blocking the enemy may not be accomplished, and collateral damage considerations may prevent the use of long-range fires in many instances. When traditional maneuver (through the current doctrine) with the BCT is used, the mission is accomplished, but with some losses; with the wide range of advanced technologies available in the time frame, losses can be reduced, but it may not be enough. New and novel, perhaps even nontraditional, doctrine and tactics would probably be required to ensure success in facing an armor threat with an FCS-based (less than 20-ton) vehicle force. Flexible air insertion has the great promise of the technology and tactical alternatives, but it also carries the great risk. Operational maneuver puts the enemy on the defensive, but survivability of the airlifters makes development of multispectral protection systems a high priority.[1]

POTENTIAL ENEMY COUNTERMEASURES

The obvious question facing any long-term technology improvement program is what the enemy can do to counter it. The responses range from deception to direct attack on vulnerable systems. In this section we look at some of the possible countermeasures in relation to the employment of long-range fires, BCT ground attack, and vertical envelopment.

Countermeasures Against Long-Range Fires (Remote Attack)

Countermeasures can be especially effective when the Blue forces are relying on standoff sensors and long-range fires. One thing the enemy could do is hide units well within tree lines or covered urban areas but with good LOS and field of fire looking outward. In this countermeasure, the enemy could use terrain for concealment, could locate itself near noncombatant buildings, or incorporate multispectral camouflage netting. Another countermeasure the enemy could employ is to use deceptive heat and acoustic sources. This could include setting up decoys with generators, heaters, and acoustics, heating destroyed vehicles with interior wood/coal fires, or establishing deceptive movements from position to position (e.g., fast movements or noncombatant vehicle movements). Finally, the enemy could employ a whole series of countermeasures, including dispensing smoke as a short-term obscurant, mounting corner reflectors on combat and noncombat vehicles, jamming Blue systems (e.g., communications, Global Positioning System, radars), and attacking UAVs aggressively with MANPADS.

A couple of points are noteworthy. First, the deceptions do not have to be perfect; techniques that save a few more units, personnel, and equipment can lead to more Blue losses later during ground attack options. Second, the techniques described are relatively inexpensive

_____
[1]We have assumed suppression of enemy forces that could be in the immediate vicinity of LZs.

and are readily available or producible. The techniques are in use throughout the world's armies and can be very effective. Generally, the techniques have a common feature of making detection and target identification more difficult for the Blue force. Under more restrictive ROE, difficult target identification may be all the enemy needs to keep the Blue force from attacking the target.

Countermeasures Against BCT Ground Attack

Other countermeasure techniques can focus on Red force survival and the destruction of Blue force assets during the BCT ground attack. First, the techniques of using extensive combined arms "strong points" (especially in urban areas that involve noncombatants) and of "hardening" targets are well known and practiced. Although these techniques are labor-intensive and require time and resources to implement, they are readily accomplished by even poor armies.

In particular, the hardening and hiding of fire support assets (cannons, mortars, and MRLs) are particularly effective because those systems can be "turned off" until needed, thus reducing their signature; as such, even if detected, they can often survive attack. Those surviving fire support systems can then make subsequent Blue force attacks costly and slow.

Another countermeasure includes preparing infantry and armor "dug-in" ambush positions. The enemy could disperse them and make them mutually supporting and could mount screening to prevent LOS thermal signatures. Other countermeasures include using cover and concealment during the resupply movement and calling on cannons, mortars, and MRLs for fire support.

Countermeasures Against Vertical Envelopment Attack

The enemy's attack on FTR lift assets is particularly dangerous for the Blue force. Simulation runs showed the Blue force losing most of the FTR fleet to the enemy's robust air defense. Finding and destroying the Red force ADA assets is particularly difficult because of the large number of MANPADS. As with all air assault operations, a great deal of risk is assumed because the Blue force flying in holds a very tenuous position and is far removed from normal supporting combat forces.

Particular countermeasures the enemy could employ include locating ADA assets to destroy the FTR during both ingress and egress, attacking LZs with long-range artillery, and directly attacking Blue forces before any lodgment can be secured.

RECOMMENDATIONS

Although it is not necessarily obvious, conducting an SSC can in some ways be more complex than conducting an MTW. As we observed in the context of this research, the capability to accomplish military objectives may come second to the conditions and constraints imposed by the SSC itself. As a result, even 15 to 20 years out, the available suite of remote sensors and precision-guided weapons is not a panacea; indeed, even had such forecasted remote capabilities been available in 1999, many of the challenges seen in Operation Allied Force would still have remained.

A new medium-weight force, such as the notional BCT considered here, represents a more direct method for responding to such challenges, providing a means for direct tactical target engagement with the ability to discriminate noncombatants. However, we note that having the ability to deploy rapidly, in and of itself, may not be enough.

For one, policy may need to be adjusted to reflect the capability of the unit itself. That is, the ability to deploy quickly may ultimately mean very little if the decision time to use the force is lengthy. Thus, if policy and guidelines are not integrated with the new capability, they can be the constraining factor. Such policy issues should be researched further.

For another, the BCT may have to have contain various technology enhancements to be successful. The key technologies identified for the notional BCT in this research were intelligence systems and tactical sensor networks; robotics-related technologies, such as advanced UAVs and unmanned ground vehicles (UGVs); weapons (both direct and indirect) that can engage through foliage; and protection systems for ground and air vehicles. These can provide considerable and needed improvement toward BCT mission effectiveness.

The most favorable outcomes, however, occurred when a joint force was used—specifically, where ground forces such as the BCT were complemented with a range of appropriate remote sensors and weapons. Although casualties are likely with the aggressive use of remote weapons, the presence of a ground force can help to mitigate this. Similarly, ground forces, without the "softening" effect of standoff engagement, were more susceptible to being ambushed and engaged by heavy armor.

We emphasize that the SSC examined here is only one of many situations that should be considered when evaluating major acquisition decisions. Other scenarios and missions should be explored in a wide range of locations. In addition, we note that only a handful of key technology areas were ultimately examined and assessed, and many of the representations we used were surrogates for the emerging BCT components. This set should certainly be expanded to include the many other ideas that are being generated. Although there will most likely be a continuing desire to resolve the SSC class of crises through remote application of force, many of the tactics and technologies associated with these kinds of engagements come with major limitations, which should be more fully evaluated and understood as the Army and DARPA pursue different joint concepts and designs for the Objective Force.

Appendix
NONCOMBATANT CASUALTIES AS A RESULT OF ALLIED ENGAGEMENTS

March 27, 2000: *The New York Times* today reported [that] on Friday, State Department officials gave reports of a forced march considerable credence . . . . They told allies the reports seemed "horribly right," a western diplomat said. *The Times* (London) cited witnesses saying "families passing in front of them heard the soldiers tell these men they will go everywhere the tanks go."

May 18, 2000: UNHCR reported today that an ethnic Albanian refugee "who arrived [Tuesday] told UNHCR that there were around 50,000 people waiting to leave the Vitina area. He reported that the military were using civilians for protection. Tanks, heavy artillery and anti-aircraft guns were reported hidden in civilian houses and barns. During NATO air strikes, he said, Yugoslav troops move as close as they can to populated areas, where they can seek protection.

INTRODUCTION AND UNDERLYING ASSUMPTIONS

The primary focus during the conduct of this study's simulation-supported analysis was the comparison of alternative munitions and delivery systems. As such, destroying specified targets—rather than cost minimization, preservation of noncombatant life, or other factors—was the focus of attention. Simulation rules of engagement (ROE) reflect this prioritization. However, the issue of noncombatant casualties significantly influenced targeting during recent air operations over Kosovo in 2000 (Operation Allied Force). It is notable that Serb forces increased their use of civilian shields as allied targeting became more successful.[1] It is very likely that concerns

---

[1]Email to Russell W. Glenn from LTC Thomas Kelley and MAJ Stephen K. Iwicki, Subject: "Army Science Board Queries for Allied Force," August 30, 2000. LTC Kelley

about noncombatant casualties will also affect U.S. operations during future contingencies. This brief supporting analysis addresses this sensitive issue, the political and strategic consequences of which could dramatically influence domestic and worldwide perceptions of an operation's success.

A designated probability of kill (P_k) of 0.8 for vehicle engagements dictated the number of rounds used to engage targets. As was noted in the body of the report, this P_k was considered fixed throughout the simulation. Target destruction therefore became a function of the number of rounds needed to attain that value. Such designation of a particular P_k had direct influence on the number of noncombatant casualties, as did the type of munitions used and the probability of injury to exposed personnel associated with each.

Assumptions used in the estimates of noncombatant losses include the following:

- Allied forces treated all noncombatants equally. For example, ROE did not distinguish between Serb Kosovars and those of Albanian extraction.

- "Densely populated" was taken to mean urban areas (with an assumed density of 1,500 persons/km^2); "sparsely populated" meant other types of terrain (assumed density of 15 persons/km^2). Unfortunately, the distances at which various munitions pose a danger to exposed personnel are rarely available for operations in urban environments. While structures surely have some shielding effect, building collapse and spalling are secondary yet major causes of injury. For the purposes of this analysis, the assumption was made that personnel close to an urban-area detonation would be as likely to suffer injury as they would be in an open environment, the shielding effects of structures being offset by the threat of collapse and flying debris. Others at a greater distance would likely benefit from the shielding provided by buildings; it was thus assumed that their injury rates would be less than for personnel in the open.

---

was the Task Force Hawk/V Corps G2 Analysis and Control Element (ACE) chief during Operation Allied Force; MAJ Iwicki was the deputy ACE chief for that organization.

- Targets were assumed to be sufficiently dispersed that bombs meant for a given target would not strike noncombatants in the vicinity of other targets. This assumption is in keeping with normal force protection procedures; separation is maintained so as to reduce the chances of multiple vehicles being lost to a single round.
- The casualty prediction statistics for unprotected personnel used in this study were based on an assumption that individuals were in a standing position. When close to a detonation, an individual's posture is less likely to affect his chances of being injured than it might at greater distances. Blast, collapse, and spalling are likely to injure an individual in virtually any posture if the detonation is at close range. However, at greater distances, an individual's efforts to reduce his exposed surface area would reduce his chances of injury. During casualty estimate calculations for those over 100 yards from a target, therefore, it was assumed that they would tend to be in a protective posture when bombs exploded. To account for this behavior and the benefits provided by structures acting as shields (as highlighted above), the probability of injury was reduced by half for civilians farther from targets. (It is understood that not all bombs hit their targets, and thus there is some error in assuming that civilians' distances from those targets equaled their offset from bomb impact points.)
- The source from which casualty statistics for this analysis were adapted did not delineate between killed and wounded. Instead, the only value given was for the probability that an individual would be "incapacitated." Unfortunately, the source document failed to define "incapacitation." It is possible that casualties would include those incapacitated (i.e., killed or badly wounded) and others suffering lesser wounds. In other words, P(wounded) = P(incapacitation) + P(lesser injury). In keeping with the team's efforts not to inflate casualty statistics, however, the probability of incapacitation was assumed to cover all casualties, i.e., P(wounded) = P(incapacitation). We would expect this and the other assumptions shown below to result in a slight underestimation of civilian injuries rather than inflated values:
    — Estimates stated that 75–80 percent of targets in urban areas were intermixed with (i.e., in close proximity to) noncombat-

ants. The equivalent value for targets in other environments was 5–10 percent. Again, to not inflate the noncombatant casualty estimates, the lower values in each case (75 and 5 percent, respectively) were used.

— When the number of rounds needed to attain a P_k of 0.8 exceeded 1,000, the conservative value of 1,000 was used.

- An apparent exception to this conservative approach is the assumption that noncombatants would be evenly distributed between the circle within 100 meters of a target [area = $\pi r^2 = \pi (100)^2 = 31,416$ m^2] and those in a ring 100 to 200 meters from the target [area = $\pi (200)^2 - \pi (100)^2 = 94248$ m^2]. (Values for probability of injury were given only for personnel up to 200 meters from detonation.)[2] However, it was felt that this provided better replication of actual conditions, since an adversary deliberately using civilians as shields would likely force them to remain close by potential targets.

Correspondence with two U.S. Army officers indicated that Serb leaders intermixed their forces with civilians more frequently in built-up areas than in rural environments.[3] This was probably due partly to the fact that when outside of towns or villages, refugees attempted to avoid Serb forces by hiding in forests, valleys, or mountains. The officers estimated that in such cases, potential targets were intermixed with noncombatants only 5–10 percent of the time; the equivalent value in villages, towns, or cities was 75–80 percent. These values obviously represent an average rather than constant value; as has been noted, deliberate intermixing by enemy forces occurred more often as allied success in engaging targets increased. For the purposes of evaluating noncombatant losses, it was assumed that 20 percent of targeted vehicles were in built-up areas, with the remainder in other environments. This 20 percent value would also have varied over time; it would probably have been lower initially and higher as an adversary sought to hide its vehicles in buildings or

---

[2]It should be noted that this limit of 200 meters is likely to reflect lower casualties for the 2,000-pound weapon than would otherwise be the case. The influence on values for the 250-pound munitions is minimal, with the possible exception of one with a CEP of 90 meters.

[3]Kelley and Iwicki.

put them close to proscribed targets, most of which are located in built-up areas.

Five hundred targets were engaged, of which 343 were hit. As noncombatants in the area could suffer wounds whether the strike was successful or not, the value of 500 was employed in determining the expected number of civilians injured.

ASSESSING THE IMPACT OF USING NONCOMBATANTS AS SHIELDS

The influence of restrictive ROE on allied targeting during Operation Allied Force was significant. Civilian casualties precipitated a ban on the use of engagements employing bomblet munitions. Concern over such injuries also precipitated other less overt but even more influential constraints on operations. The deputy ACE chief for TF Hawk summed it up as follows:

> What effect did large numbers of civilians on the battlefield [have] on our operations? The answer is that it was very significant. We had to adopt a new approach to targeting that included tracking civilian concentrations, clearing targets of civilians prior to target execution, and many other facets that are not part of our military doctrine. This requirement was a major consumer of personnel, time, and intelligence collectors to ensure that the targets nominated and Air Force engaged were not only valid but would not have ANY collateral damage (mainly civilians). While we did pretty good tracking civilian concentrations, it was not perfect or close to real time information. This resulted in a number of valid and significant military ground mobile targets going unstruck.[4]

Given that noncombatant casualties have become a matter of strategic concern, selection of a given system or munition type should reasonably include consideration of the collateral damage consequences of that choice. Determination of such consequences relies on a number of factors. First, the influence of noncombatant losses is not constant. It is greater if the injuries are incurred on U.S. or an allied nation's territory. There may also be what is, to this

---

[4]Ibid. Comments are those of MAJ Iwicki.

point, a little-understood relationship between friendly force casualties and noncombatant losses. Given the alternatives of large numbers of friendly forces lost versus similar or larger numbers of noncombatants killed or wounded, it is possible that the consequences of choosing the latter would be less damaging in terms of domestic public support. It is unlikely, however, that public opinion in the near term will tolerate significant numbers of civilian deaths as a consequence of engagements by U.S. forces during which American losses are very limited. There is need for further research in this area.

OBSERVATIONS

Information on such factors as the location of civilian concentrations in Kosovo at any given time, the percentage of potential targets with noncombatants in the vicinity, the effects of munitions on exposed personnel in villages, towns, and cities, and other matters of concern was often not available. However, both commercial and military information sources confirm that noncombatants were frequently in proximity to legitimate military targets. This juxtaposition was at times coincidental but, as has been noted, at other times was the result of deliberate efforts by Serb forces to use civilians as shields against allied attack. That the West, and in particular the United States, desires to minimize casualties among innocents is common knowledge. That future adversaries will use this hesitancy to engage civilian targets is a given.

CALCULATION OF NONCOMBATANT CASUALTIES

Review of Assumptions Underlying Calculations

- 20 percent of targets engaged were in urban areas, 80 percent in rural areas.

- 75 percent of targets in urban areas had noncombatants in vicinity; 5 percent of targets in rural areas had noncombatants in vicinity.

- Total number of targets engaged was 500. Therefore, $(500)(.20) = 100$ targets were assumed to be in urban areas; $(500)(.80) = 400$ were in rural areas.

- Distribution of targets (based on unclassified values for Operation Allied Force):
  — Hard targets: 10 percent
  — Medium targets: 25 percent
  — Soft targets: 65 percent

  Therefore, the number of targets with noncombatants in the vicinity, by type of target, was as shown in the table below. For example, the number of hard targets in urban areas is (100 total urban targets) × (.75 urban targets with noncombatants in vicinity) × (.10 of all targets were hard targets) = 7.5 → 8 hard targets in urban areas with noncombatants in the vicinity.

  Number of Targets with Noncombatants in Vicinity, by Type, in Urban and Rural Terrain (Numbers Rounded Up to Next Whole Number)

Target Type	Urban	Rural
Hard	8	2
Medium	19	5
Soft	49	13

- Assumed TLE: 3 meters.
- Noncombatants were assumed to be distributed over a 200-meter radius circle around each target such that 50 percent were within 100 meters of the target and the remaining half were from 100 to 200 meters of the target. The probability of injury to individuals within a particular group (where the groups were (1) those within or at 100 meters from a target or (2) those more than 100 and up to 200 meters from a target) was assumed to be constant for each group. In other words, all civilians within 100 meters of a target were assumed to have the same probability of being injured.
- The probability of injury for those outside the 100-meter distance was reduced by half to account for shielding and protective postures assumed by exposed personnel.
- Probability values for civilians 100 meters or less from targets were computed by averaging the probabilities of injury for un-

protected personnel at 25, 50, 75, and 100 meters from the target. Note that because of the assumption that noncombatants were forced to stay close to targets, the probability of noncombatant injury *decreases* as weapon accuracy decreases. However, the larger number of bombs that had to be dropped in order to achieve a P_k of 0.8 mitigated any such apparent "benefits" of bomb inaccuracy.

Determination of Expected Number of Noncombatant Casualty Values

Probability of Injury for Unprotected Personnel by Weapon Type

Distance from Target	Weapon				
	2,000-lb 3m CEP	250-lb 3m CEP	250-lb 10m CEP	250-lb 15m CEP	250-lb 90m CEP
≤100 m	.83	.55	.51	.47	.06
>100–200 m	.095	0	.005	.005	.025

To determine the number of noncombatants injured for each of these cases (urban or rural; engagement of hard, medium, or soft target), it is necessary to identify the number of bombs or other munitions needed to achieve a P_k of 0.8. These values are as follows:

Number of Munitions of Given Type to Achieve $P_k = 0.8$ by Type of Target

Target Type	Weapon				
	2,000-lb 3m CEP	250-lb 3m CEP	250-lb 10m CEP	250-lb 15m CEP	250-lb 90m CEP*
Hard	3.9	4.5	26.0	52.8	>1,000
Medium	1.0	2.7	12.6	26.0	>1,000
Soft	1.0	2.9	17.1	39.4	>1,000

*As stated previously, 1,000 engagements was the value used when determining the number of casualties due to the employment of 250-pound munitions with a CEP of 90 meters.

Determination of the number of expected casualties for each target engagement is a function of the probability of injury by weapon type, the number of times a target must be engaged to achieve the designated P_k, and the number of noncombatants within the area in which they could be wounded. The formula used to determine the total number of casualties for each case is therefore

Expected casualties = [1 − (probability of civilians not being injured)$^{\text{number of rounds}}$] × (number of noncombatants within range) × (number of targets),

first calculating the relevant probabilities using

[1 − (probability of civilians not being injured)$^{\text{number of rounds}}$].

Expected Percentage of Noncombatants Injured Per Engagement by Target Type and Weapon in Urban Terrain

Target Type (urban)	Weapon				
	2,000-lb 3m CEP	250-lb 3m CEP	250-lb 10m CEP	250-lb 15m CEP	250-lb 90m CEP
Hard	100 (16.1)	97.2 (0)	100 (6.1)	100 (11.6)	100 (50)
Medium	83 (4.75)	88.4 (0)	100 (3.1)	100 (6.1)	100 (50)
Soft	83 (4.75)	90.1 (0)	100 (4.1)	100 (9.0)	100 (50)

First value is for personnel 100 meters or less from the target; value in parentheses is for those beyond 100 meters but less than 200 meters from the target.

Using the assumed value of 1,500 persons/km² for an urban (densely populated) area, the average number of civilians within a 200-meter radius from a target is 188.5, half of whom are assumed to be 0 to 100 meters from the target, the remainder 100 to 200 meters away. In this case, the total number of noncombatants exposed to injury would be equal to the (number of targets of each type) × (number of civilians within a 200-meter circle) = (number of targets of each type) × (188.5).

74   Exploring Technologies for the Future Combat Systems Program

Possible Noncombatant Casualties in Urban Engagements, by Target Type

Target Type	Number of Targets	Number of Noncombatants	Total Noncombatants Exposed to Injury
Hard	8	188.5	1,508
Medium	19	188.5	3,582
Soft	49	188.5	9,237

The total possible casualties (summing the final column) is 14,327. Using the formula given above, the expected number of casualties resulting from the engagement of all urban targets for each type of weapon is as shown below. The first value in each cell is the number injured for personnel 100 meters or less from the target; the value in parentheses is for those between 100 and 200 meters from the target.

Expected Number of Noncombatant Casualties for Density of 1,500 Persons Per Square Kilometer (Densely Populated/Urban Terrain)

Target Type (urban)	Weapon				
	2,000-lb 3m CEP	250-lb 3m CEP	250-lb 10m CEP	250-lb 15m CEP	250-lb 90m CEP
Hard	753 (121)	735 (0)	754 (46)	754 (87)	754 (377)
Medium	1,486 (85)	1,583 (0)	1,791 (56)	1,791 (109)	1,791 (895)
Soft	3,833 (219)	4,161 (0)	4,618 (189)	4,618 (416)	4,618 (2,309)
Total injured	6,497	6,479	7,454	7,775	10,744

In this case, given the assumptions noted above, the 250-pound bomb with a 3-meter CEP results in the fewest noncombatant casualties (6,479, or 45.2 percent of the 14,327 total possible casualties). A 2000-pound bomb with a 3-meter CEP is only marginally more harmful in this regard, with 6,497 casualties (45.3 percent), though it must be remembered that the artificiality of only giving the probability of casualties out to 200 meters does not reflect those beyond this range who would be injured with this larger bomb. The most damaging to noncombatants was the least accurate 250-pound bomb (CEP = 90 meters), with 10,744 injured (75.0 percent of total possible). Calculations pertaining to noncombatant losses resulting from attacks on targets in rural (sparsely populated) terrain would be determined in a similar manner.

BIBLIOGRAPHY

"Armored Cavalry Regiment (ACR) Combat Units," *Periscope's USNI Military Database*, July 3, 1995.

Bugajski, Janusz, "Problems of Balkan Reconstruction," testimony delivered before the House Committee on International Relations, U.S. Congress, Washington D.C., August 4, 1999.

Collins, Joseph J., "10 Reasons to Avoid a Land War," *The Boston Globe*, May 23, 1999.

Cook, Nick, "War of Extremes," *Jane's Defence Weekly*, October 4, 1999.

Cordesman, Anthony H., *Notes on a Land Option in Kosovo*, Washington D.C.: Center for Strategic and International Studies, April 26, 1999.

Cordesman, Anthony H., *Yugoslav Military and Security Forces: Facts and Figures*, Washington D.C.: Center for Strategic and International Studies, revised April 22, 1999.

Cunningham, Bruce J., and Raymond P. Gogolewski, *An Annotated Briefing: Preliminary Thoughts on Lightweight Armored Fighting Vehicles*, briefing charts, Livermore, Calif.: Lawrence Livermore National Laboratory, UCID-21626, December 23, 1988, limited distribution.

Dunlap, Charles J., Jr., "Technology: Recomplicating Moral Life for the Nation's Defenders," *Parameters*, Autumn 1999, pp. 24–53.

Freedberg, Sydney J., Jr., "The New-Model Army," *National Journal*, June 3, 2000, p. 1750.

Ingram, Michael C., and E. Thomas Powers, *Army After Next (AAN) FY99 Tactical Excursions, Final Report*, U.S. Army Training and Doctrine Command Fort Monroe, VA: Deputy Chief of Staff for Doctrine, TRAC-TR-0999, April 30, 2000.

Kendall, Frank and Paul Funk (Co-Chairpersons of Army Science Board), *Full-Spectrum Protection for 2025-Era Ground Combat Vehicles*, final report, briefing charts, FY99 Army Science Board Summer Study, July 22, 1999.

Killebrew, Robert B., "Army Force Projection," *Armed Forces Journal International*, September 1999, pp. 90–96.

"Kosovo Sector Responsibilities," *Defense Link*, June 1999.

Laurenzo, Ron, "Army May Accelerate Fielding of Medium Force," *Defense Week*, Vol. 20, No. 37, September 20, 1999, p. 1.

Leaf, Tim, "Thermobaric Weapons: A Weapon of Choice for Urban Warfare," Marine Corps Intelligence Activity, MCIA-1142-0001-99, August 1999, unclassified.

Ministry of National Defense, "Yugoslavia (Serbia and Montenegro)," *World Armies*, Serbia, n.d.

Naylor, Sean D., "Combining Arms, Can One Combat Vehicle Do It All? The Army's Betting on It," *Army Times*, August 30, 1999, pp. 14–15.

Office of the Deputy Chief of Staff for Doctrine, Headquarters U.S. Army Training and Doctrine Command, "Army Transformation Wargame 2000," pamphlet, n.d.

"Satellite Pictures: Private Eyes in the Sky," *The Economist*, May 6, 2000, pp. 71–73.

Stevens, R., *CSA's Vision—Implications and Dependencies*, January 14, 2000, working draft.

"USA—Unit Organization—Army—USNI Military Database," *Periscope's USNI Military Database*, July 3, 1995.

Zahn, Brian R., *The Future Combat System: Minimizing Risk While Maximizing Capability*, Carlisle Barracks, PA: U.S. Army War College, April 24, 2000, SSP Working Paper.